Best of the Best

the best recipes from the **25** best cookbooks of the year

from the editors of

FOOD & WINE BEST OF THE BEST VOL. 9
EDITOR **Kate Heddings**
ART DIRECTOR **Liz Quan**
DESIGNER **Nancy Blumberg**
SENIOR EDITOR **Rachael Philipps Shapiro**
COPY EDITOR **Carmen Armillas**
ASSISTANT EDITOR **Melissa Rubel**
PRODUCTION MANAGER **Matt Carson**
REPORTERS **Kristin Donnelly, Catherine Jang, Kalina Mazur, Jen Murphy, Stacey Nield, Jessica Tzerman**

FOOD & WINE MAGAZINE
EDITOR IN CHIEF **Dana Cowin**
CREATIVE DIRECTOR **Stephen Scoble**
MANAGING EDITOR **Mary Ellen Ward**
EXECUTIVE EDITOR **Pamela Kaufman**
EXECUTIVE FOOD EDITOR **Tina Ujlaki**
ART DIRECTOR **Patricia Sanchez**

AMERICAN EXPRESS PUBLISHING CORPORATION
SENIOR VICE PRESIDENT, CHIEF MARKETING OFFICER **Mark V. Stanich**
VICE PRESIDENT, BOOKS AND PRODUCTS **Marshall Corey**
PRODUCTION DIRECTOR **Rosalie Abatemarco-Samat**
CORPORATE PRODUCTION MANAGER **Stuart N. Handelman**
SENIOR MARKETING MANAGER **Bruce Spanier**
ASSISTANT MARKETING MANAGER **Sarah Ross**
SENIOR OPERATIONS MANAGER **Phil Black**
BUSINESS MANAGER **Thomas Noonan**

COVER
PHOTOGRAPH BY Tina Rupp
FOOD STYLING BY Alison Attenborough
PROP STYLING BY Alistair Turnball
FLAP PHOTOGRAPHS
DANA COWIN PORTRAIT BY Andrew French
KATE HEDDINGS PORTRAIT BY Andrew French

ISBN 1-932624-14-7
ISSN 1524-2862

Published by American Express Publishing Corporation
1120 Avenue of the Americas, New York, New York 10036

Manufactured in the United States of America

Best of the Best

the best recipes from the **25** best cookbooks of the year

FOOD&WINE
BOOKS

American Express Publishing Corporation, New York

MANGOES & CURRY LEAVES
CULINARY TRAVELS THROUGH THE GREAT SUBCONTINENT

JEFFREY ALFORD AND NAOMI DUGUID

MOLTO ITALIANO
MARIO BATALI

Rick Bayless
MEXICAN EVERYDAY
EASY · FULL-FLAVORED · TRADITION-PACKED

More than 175 Recipes from Spain's Hottest Chefs and Finest Cooks
LA COCINA DE MAMÁ
The Great Home Cooking of Spain
Penelope Casas
Author of TAPAS

Chef interrupted
Delicious chefs' recipes that you can actually make at home

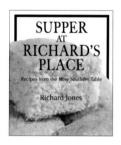
THE NEW YORK TIMES BESTSELLER
125 SIMPLE AND DELICIOUS RECIPES
everydayitalian
GIADA DE LAURENTIIS

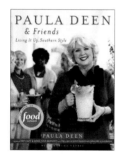
PAULA DEEN & Friends
Living It Up, Southern Style
PAULA DEEN

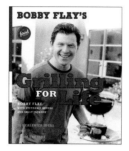
BOBBY FLAY'S
Grilling FOR Life
BOBBY FLAY WITH STEPHANIE BANYAS AND SALLY JACKSON

tyler florence
eat THIS BOOK
COOKING WITH GLOBAL FRESH FLAVOR

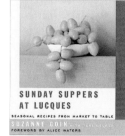
SUNDAY SUPPERS AT LUCQUES
SEASONAL RECIPES FROM MARKET TO TABLE
SUZANNE GOIN
FOREWORD BY ALICE WATERS

SUPPER AT RICHARD'S PLACE
Recipes from the New Southern Table
Richard Jones

small bites
flavors, sushi, meze, antipasti and other finger foods
Jennifer Joyce

eating korean
from barbecue to kimchi, recipes from my home
CECILIA HAE-JIN LEE

★BRUNCH★
100 RECIPES FROM FIVE POINTS RESTAURANT
MARC MEYER AND PETER MEEHAN
UNIVERSE

CHOCOLATE OBSESSION
MICHAEL RECCHIUTI & FRAN GAGE

Galatoire's COOKBOOK

SEASONED IN THE SOUTH
RECIPES FROM CROOK'S CORNER AND FROM HOME
BILL SMITH WITH A MEMOIR BY LEE SMITH

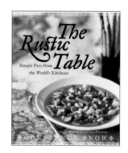
The Rustic Table
Simple Fare from the World's Kitchens

RECIPES
a collection for the modern cook
Susan Spungen
Foreword by Martha Stewart

Sweet Gratitude
bake a thank-you for the really important people in your life
Judith Sutton

the HERBAL KITCHEN
COOKING WITH FRAGRANCE AND FLAVOR
JERRY TRAUNFELD

The NEW SPANISH TABLE
Anya von Bremzen

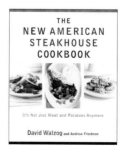
THE NEW AMERICAN STEAKHOUSE COOKBOOK
It's Not Just Meat and Potatoes Anymore
David Walzog and Andrew Friedman

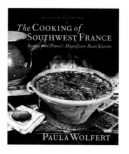
The COOKING of SOUTHWEST FRANCE
Recipes from France's Magnificent Rustic Cuisine
PAULA WOLFERT

chocolate
LISA YOCKELSON

Contents

Contents continued

Recipes

Foreword

We at FOOD & WINE often hear from readers who think they can't cook, citing failed attempts at making recipes from cookbooks. The truth is that these people are probably very able in the kitchen, but they're sabotaged by flawed recipes. When we began testing cookbooks for *Best of the Best,* we started with 250 contenders, then weeded out the disappointments to find the 25 that deserve a place in our canon. These are reliable, delightful, exciting books you can turn to for a dinner party, weeknight meal or baking session with complete confidence.

Michael Recchiuti's *Chocolate Obsession* is a stunning work by a master chocolate artisan. With help from co-author Fran Gage, Recchiuti clearly describes how to create extraordinary desserts like Burnt Caramel Pots de Crème. Jeffrey Alford and Naomi Duguid's *Mangoes & Curry Leaves* teaches the everyday cooking of the Indian subcontinent, with recipes like Baked Goan Fish with Fresh Green Chile Chutney that are novel yet comfortingly simple. And Bill Smith's *Seasoned in the South* is a wonderful glimpse into his kitchen, with its funny, heartfelt tales and stupendous recipes. We will definitely be preparing his Green Peach Salad and Green Tabasco Chicken at home.

To make *Best of the Best* even better, we've gone to many of these star cookbook authors and persuaded them to part with a special, never-before-published recipe. We urge you to try Melissa Clark's smart and appealing Shredded Brussels Sprouts Salad with Walnuts and Manchego and Anya von Bremzen's supereasy Georgian Cheese Pie.

We want you to cook each and every recipe in this unique collection with complete success! Please e-mail us at cookbookcomments@aexp.com to let us know how you do.

Dana Cowin
Editor in Chief
FOOD & WINE MAGAZINE

Kate Heddings
Editor
FOOD & WINE COOKBOOKS

Sri Lankan Beef Curry, p. 14

Mangoes & Curry Leaves

by Jeffrey Alford and Naomi Duguid

Toronto-based authors Jeffrey Alford and Naomi Duguid have traveled throughout Asia for 30 years, studying, photographing, eating and immersing themselves in the culture. Here they focus on the everyday cooking of the Indian subcontinent—the memorable dishes they discovered in neighborhood restaurants and village homes in India, Pakistan, Bangladesh, Nepal and Sri Lanka. A thrilling book for the confident cook.

Published by Artisan, 384 pages, $45.

Find more recipes by Jeffrey Alford and Naomi Duguid at **foodandwine.com/ alfordduguid**

Sri Lankan Beef Curry

The curry leaves and green chile give this Sri Lankan curry a pretty pale green color. We use either boneless beef or ribs, and you can also use the same method to make lamb curry (see the variation). The dish has plenty of aromatic sauce slightly enriched with coconut milk, and a mild chile heat. Leftovers are delicious.

SERVES 4 TO 5

- 1 pound boneless beef (such as round steaks or roast) or about 1½ pounds short ribs or cross ribs
- 1 tablespoon vegetable oil

About 10 fresh or frozen curry leaves

- 1 green cayenne chile, finely chopped

Generous 1 cup finely chopped onion

- 1 teaspoon turmeric
- 1 teaspoon salt
- ½ cup canned or fresh coconut milk
- 1 tablespoon tamarind pulp
- ¼ cup hot water
- 3 cups water

DRY SPICE MIXTURE

- 1 tablespoon raw white rice
- 1 tablespoon coriander seeds
- 1 teaspoon cumin seeds

One 1-inch piece cinnamon or cassia stick

- 5 to 6 cardamom seeds (from 1 to 2 green cardamom pods)

Cut the boneless beef into approximately ½-inch cubes. Or, if using ribs, cut them apart. Set aside.

In a small dry heavy skillet, roast the dry spice mixture over medium-high heat for 3 to 4 minutes, stirring frequently, until it has a good aroma. Transfer to a spice/coffee grinder and grind to a powder, or grind with a mortar and a pestle. Set aside in a small bowl.

In a wide heavy pot, heat the oil over medium-high heat. When the oil is hot, add the curry leaves, green chile, onion, and turmeric and stir-fry for 3 minutes. Add the beef and salt and cook, stirring occasionally to expose all surfaces of the meat to the hot oil, for 5 minutes, or until the meat is browned.

Add the reserved dry spice mixture and the coconut milk and stir to coat the meat with the coconut milk. Reduce the heat to medium and cook for 10 minutes, stirring occasionally.

Meanwhile, chop the tamarind pulp and soak it in the hot water for about 10 minutes. Press the mixture through a strainer or sieve placed over a bowl. Discard the pulp and combine the tamarind liquid with the 3 cups water.

Add the liquid to the pot and bring to a boil, then lower the heat and cook at a strong simmer for about 1 hour, or until the meat is tender and the flavors well blended.

Taste and adjust the seasoning, if you wish. Serve hot.

Serve with plenty of rice to soak up the sauce and with a sweet chutney.

SRI LANKAN LAMB CURRY Lamb makes another wonderful version of this curry. The slight acidity of the sauce complements the sweetness of the lamb. Use 1 pound boneless lamb shoulder, trimmed of fat.

duguid on short ribs

Short ribs aren't a traditional cut of meat for this dish, but they taste great. You sort of think that if someone had been making this dish in Sri Lanka and then they came to North America and discovered short ribs, they'd adapt the recipe. People do that all the time.

Cucumber Salad with
Hot Spiced Mustard Dressing

SERVES 3 TO 4

½ pound cucumbers, preferably a small English cucumber, peeled

Kosher salt

1 tablespoon sesame seeds

½ teaspoon cumin seeds

2 tablespoons plain (full- or reduced-fat) yogurt or water

1½ teaspoons mustard oil

⅛ teaspoon fenugreek seeds

⅛ teaspoon nigella seeds

1 green cayenne chile, slit lengthwise and seeded

¼ teaspoon cayenne

⅛ teaspoon turmeric

1 tablespoon fresh lemon juice

2 to 3 tablespoons minced coriander leaves

Cut the cucumber lengthwise in quarters. Slice off the seeds (unless the cucumbers are very small and tender) and discard, then cut into 1½-inch lengths. Cut lengthwise in half again if the pieces are fat. Place in a colander, sprinkle on about 2 tablespoons kosher salt, and set over a bowl or in the sink to drain for 15 minutes.

Meanwhile, in a heavy skillet, dry roast the sesame seeds until golden. Transfer to a plate and set aside. Dry roast the cumin seeds until touched with color and aromatic, then transfer to a spice/coffee grinder, add the sesame seeds, and grind to a powder. Place in a small bowl and stir in the yogurt or water to make a paste. Set aside.

Rinse the cucumbers thoroughly with cold water. Squeeze them gently to squeeze out excess water and place them in a bowl. Add the spice paste and rub the cucumbers all over to coat them. Set aside.

Heat the oil in a small skillet over medium heat. Add the fenugreek, nigella, and chile and cook for about a minute, stirring occasionally, until the spices are aromatic. Add the cayenne and turmeric, stir, and pour the flavored oil over the cucumbers; toss gently. Add the lemon juice and toss, then set aside for 10 to 20 minutes to allow the flavors to blend.

Just before serving, add the coriander leaves and ½ teaspoon salt, or more to taste, and toss gently to mix.

duguid on food processors

I love making things by hand, but we do use the food processor for unleavened bread doughs because it's so easy. You can make *chapati* in an instant. Put all the ingredients in the mixer and— boom—it's ready.

Spiced Grated Carrots, Kerala Style

editor's note

Alford and Duguid explain that this side dish would be one of several served with rice at the noontime main meal in Kerala. The recipe is an *oleete*, a category of vegetable dish that is stir-fried, then mixed with yogurt as it finishes cooking.

SERVES 4

2 tablespoons raw sesame oil or vegetable oil

1 teaspoon black mustard seeds

About ½ cup minced onion

¼ teaspoon turmeric

1 tablespoon minced ginger or ginger mashed to a paste

2 green cayenne chiles, slit lengthwise and seeded

About 10 fresh or frozen curry leaves

3 to 4 medium carrots, coarsely grated (about 1½ cups)

½ teaspoon salt, or more to taste

Coarsely ground black pepper (optional)

About ½ cup plain yogurt, preferably full-fat

Heat the oil in a medium heavy skillet or a wok or *karhai* (see below) over medium-high heat. Add the mustard seeds and partially cover until they pop, then add the onion and turmeric and stir-fry for 2 minutes. Add the ginger, chiles, and curry leaves and stir-fry until the onion is very soft, about another 5 minutes. Toss in the carrots, salt, and pepper, if using. Stir-fry for about 5 minutes, or until the carrots are very soft.

Turn the heat to very low. Add the yogurt and stir for a minute or so to warm the yogurt through and blend flavors; do not allow it to boil.

Serve in a shallow bowl.

KARHAI A *karhai* (sometimes transcribed *kadhai* or *karahi*; pronounced "ka-'rye") is a traditional woklike cooking pot with two handles; in Britain, it has recently come to be called a *Balti pan*. Anthropologists and archeologists say that it may be the precursor of the Chinese wok. It is used for stir-frying and simmering many dishes. A wok, heavy skillet, or wide heavy pot can be substituted.

Baked Goan Fish with Fresh Green Chile Chutney

SERVES 4

One 1¾- to 2-pound firm-fleshed fish, such as pickerel, trout, or red
    snapper, cleaned and scaled
About ¼ cup vegetable oil
About 2 tablespoons fresh lime or lemon juice
About 1 tablespoon fine sea salt
About ½ cup Fresh Green Chile Chutney (recipe follows),
    plus extra to serve as a condiment

Place a rack in the center of the oven and preheat the oven to 400°F.

Wash and dry the fish. Cut a slit along each side of the backbone down the
length of the fish. Place a large sheet of foil on a rimmed baking sheet (or in
a large roasting pan). Pour about 3 tablespoons oil on the part of the sheet
where the fish will lie, and set near your work surface.

Rub the fish all over with the lime or lemon juice, then with the salt. Stuff some
of the chutney into the slits and put the remainder in the fish's cavity. Lay the
fish on the foil. Pour on the remaining 1 tablespoon oil and spread it over the
top of the fish. Wrap the foil fairly tightly around the fish; use another piece of
foil if necessary to ensure that the package is well sealed.

Bake for about 30 minutes; time will depend on the size and thickness of the
fish. To test, peel back the foil a little and press on the flesh at the thickest
part of the fish. It should yield a little and feel soft. The other test is to unwrap
more of the fish and test the texture of the flesh: If the flesh flakes with a fork,
it is cooked.

Serve the fish warm or at room temperature, with extra chutney alongside as a
condiment. Serve by lifting sections of the top fillet off the bone; when the first
side is finished, flip the fish over to serve the second fillet.

To serve the fish warm, open the foil and let stand for 10 minutes, then transfer
the fish to a platter (flip it off the foil). Pour the pan juices into a small jug, so
they can be drizzled onto each serving. Alternatively, let the fish cool to room

temperature with the foil open, then wrap again tightly in the foil and refrigerate overnight, or for at least 4 hours. When it is chilled, the pan juices around the fish thicken to a jelly, beautiful bright green in color and with a wonderful flavor blend; the fish is firm and holds its shape well. Bring back just to room temperature before serving.

Fresh Green Chile Chutney

MAKES A GENEROUS 1 CUP

About 2 cups coriander leaves and stems
  6 green cayenne chiles, coarsely chopped
  6 to 10 medium garlic cloves, chopped
  2 teaspoons minced ginger or ginger mashed to a paste
About 1 cup fresh or frozen grated coconut
  1 teaspoon cumin seeds
About 3 tablespoons fresh lime juice, or substitute lemon juice
  1 teaspoon sugar
  1 teaspoon salt, or to taste

Place the coriander, chiles, garlic, and ginger in a food processor and process to a paste. Add the coconut and process to incorporate. Transfer to a bowl.

Briefly grind the cumin seeds with a mortar and a pestle or a spice/coffee grinder, not to a powder but to crush them a little, then add to the chile mixture. Stir in the lime (or lemon) juice, sugar, and salt, then taste for salt and adjust as necessary. Serve or use immediately, or refrigerate, covered, until ready to serve. The chutney will keep for about 4 days in a well-sealed container in the refrigerator.

**Mangoes &
Curry Leaves**

JEFFREY ALFORD AND
NAOMI DUGUID

BEST OF THE BEST EXCLUSIVE

Vietnamese Subs with Vinegared Carrots

6 SERVINGS

- 1 pound carrots
- ½ teaspoon kosher salt
- 1½ cups water
- ¼ cup rice vinegar
- 2 tablespoons sugar
- 6 long French rolls, halved lengthwise, or 2 long baguettes, each split lengthwise and cut into 3 sections

Unsalted butter and mayonnaise, for spreading

- 2 tablespoons minced Thai bird chile
- ¾ pound country pâté or thinly sliced mortadella or cured ham
- 2 cups cilantro sprigs

1. Finely julienne the carrots on a mandoline or coarsely grate them on a box grater. In a colander, toss the carrots with the salt. Let stand in the sink for 30 minutes to drain. Rinse the carrots and squeeze dry, then transfer to a bowl.

2. In a small saucepan, combine the water with the vinegar and sugar and bring to a boil, stirring until the sugar dissolves. Remove from the heat and let cool to room temperature. Pour the dressing over the carrots and stir gently. Let the carrots stand for at least 1 hour.

3. Drain the carrots. Spread the cut sides of each roll with butter and mayonnaise. Sprinkle the minced chile on the bottom half of each roll and top with some of the vinegared carrots. Spread the pâté on each sandwich or arrange the sliced meats on the rolls. Top with the cilantro sprigs. Close the sandwiches, press them together firmly and serve.

editor's note

The lightly pickled carrot condiment in this sandwich is tasty with the rich pâté and sliced meats, but it can also stand on its own as a palate-refreshing side salad.

Baked Pasta with Ricotta and Ham, p. 24

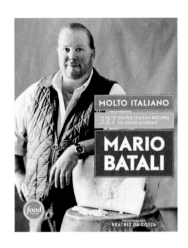

Molto Italiano

by Mario Batali

Superstar chef Mario Batali has compiled more than 300 recipes from all over Italy, from 10 years of his *Molto Mario* TV show as well as from his extensive travels. Beautiful and incredibly easy to navigate and use, the book is peppered with Batali's humor, tips and historic references. Best of all are those swoon-inducing recipes: Baked Pasta with Ricotta and Ham, for instance, and Pork Chops with Peppers and Capers.

Published by Ecco, 528 pages, $34.95.

Find more recipes by
Mario Batali at
foodandwine.com/batali

Baked Pasta with Ricotta and Ham

Pasticcio di Maccheroni

batali on the best ingredients
When I'm making this recipe, I prefer to use De Cecco or Barilla ziti. For provolone, I like a slightly aged one. And the Italian cooked ham? I like parmacotto.

Pasticcio is a full-on party for Easter—in one beautiful mess (*pasticcio*). No problem serving it *tièpido*, at room temperature.

MAKES 8 SERVINGS

  3 tablespoons extra-virgin olive oil
  1 pound Italian cooked ham, preferably parmacotto, cut into ½-inch cubes
Salt and freshly ground black pepper
  1 small carrot, cut into ¼-inch dice
  1 onion, cut into ¼-inch dice
  1 rib celery, thinly sliced
  1 cup dry red wine
1½ cups Basic Tomato Sauce (recipe follows)
1½ pounds ziti
  1 pound fresh ricotta
  8 ounces caciotta or hard provolone, cut into small dice
  ½ cup freshly grated Parmigiano-Reggiano

1. In a Dutch oven, heat the olive oil over high heat until smoking. Add the ham cubes and brown for 5 to 6 minutes. Season with salt and pepper. Add the carrot, onion, and celery and cook until the vegetables are golden brown, about 10 minutes.

2. Add the wine, bring to a boil, and cook until reduced by half, about 5 minutes. Add the tomato sauce and bring to a boil, then reduce the heat to low, cover the pan, and cook until the meat is just about falling apart, about 50 minutes. Transfer the meat to a large bowl. Keep the sauce warm.

3. Meanwhile, preheat the oven to 450°F. Bring 6 quarts of water to a boil in a large pot, and add 2 tablespoons salt.

4. Cook the ziti in the boiling water for 1 minute less than the package directions, until still very al dente. While the pasta is cooking, place the ricotta in a small bowl and stir in a ladle of the pasta cooking water to "melt" it.

5. Drain the pasta and add it to the bowl with the meat. In another bowl, add the ricotta, caciotta, and tomato sauce and stir to combine.

6. Grease a round 12-inch deep pie dish or a casserole with olive oil. Place a ladleful of the cheese and sauce mixture in the bottom of the dish, followed by a layer of the pasta and meat mixture. Sprinkle 2 to 3 tablespoons of the Parmigiano over, then repeat with another layer of the cheese and sauce mixture, then pasta and meat, and Parmigiano. Continue until all the ingredients are used up.

7. Bake for 25 minutes, until bubbling and heated through. Serve in warmed pasta bowls.

Basic Tomato Sauce
Pomodoro

MAKES 4 CUPS

¼ cup extra-virgin olive oil
 1 Spanish onion, cut into ¼-inch dice
 4 cloves garlic, thinly sliced
 3 tablespoons chopped fresh thyme
½ medium carrot, finely shredded
Two 28-ounce cans whole tomatoes
Salt

1. In a 3-quart saucepan, heat the olive oil over medium heat. Add the onion and garlic and cook until soft and light golden brown, 8 to 10 minutes. Add the thyme and carrot and cook until the carrot is quite soft, about 5 minutes.

2. Add the tomatoes, with their juice, and bring to a boil, stirring often. Lower the heat and simmer until as thick as hot cereal, about 30 minutes. Season with salt. The sauce can be refrigerated for up to 1 week or frozen for 6 months.

Sweet-and-Sour Pumpkin
Zucca in Agrodolce

This can be a side dish, a pasta sauce, and even a dessert in my world, with a little sour cream or yogurt. I love my first taste of the pungent chile-flecked sweet squash in the autumn; it means that summer is just about gone and that the really intense cooking is headed my way.

MAKES 4 SERVINGS

- ¼ cup extra-virgin olive oil
- 1 pound sugar pumpkin or acorn squash, peeled, seeded, and cut into 1-inch cubes
- 4 cloves garlic, thinly sliced
- 1 teaspoon hot red pepper flakes
- 3 tablespoons red wine vinegar
- 3 tablespoons honey
- 3 tablespoons roughly chopped fresh mint

1. In a 10- to 12-inch sauté pan, heat the olive oil over medium-high heat until smoking. Add the pumpkin and garlic and cook until the pumpkin is light golden brown, 4 to 5 minutes. Add the red pepper flakes, vinegar, and honey and bring to a boil. Reduce the heat and simmer until the liquid is reduced to a syrupy glaze and the pumpkin is tender, 10 to 12 minutes.

2. Remove from the heat, add the mint, and serve.

batali on peeling squash

If you can't find an acorn squash, you can always use a butternut squash, which is much easier to peel anyway. But if you do use an acorn squash, there's a trick to peeling it: Cut it into 1-inch-thick rounds and then just cut off the skin with a knife. Don't try to use a peeler because you'll cut your knuckles off!

Pork Chops with Peppers and Capers

Cotolette alla Zingara

Zingara translates as "gypsy," and here the name must be because of the lusty, colorful components of this fiery, festive dish.

MAKES 6 SERVINGS

4½ quarts water
  1 cup kosher salt
  1 cup packed brown sugar
 12 black peppercorns
  4 bay leaves
  6 pork rib chops
Salt and freshly ground black pepper
  1 cup all-purpose flour
  3 tablespoons extra-virgin olive oil
  3 bell peppers—1 each of red, green, and yellow—cored, seeded, and cut into thin strips
  5 bulb onions, green tops reserved and sliced, bulbs cut into rings
  ¼ cup black olives, pitted and chopped
  1 tablespoon hot red pepper flakes
  1 tablespoon capers, with their brine
  1 cup dry white wine

1. In a small saucepan, combine 2 cups of the water, the kosher salt, brown sugar, peppercorns, and bay leaves and bring to a boil over high heat, stirring to dissolve the salt and sugar. Pour into a large pot or other container and add the remaining 4 quarts cool water. Stir to mix well, add the pork chops, cover, and refrigerate overnight (see Brining, page 30).

2. Drain the chops and pat dry with paper towels. Season the pork on both sides with salt and pepper, then dredge in the flour.

3. In a 12-inch sauté pan, heat the olive oil over high heat until smoking. Add 3 chops to the pan and cook until dark golden brown on the first side, about 7 minutes. Turn over and cook until browned on the second side, about 4 minutes, then transfer to a plate and repeat with the other 3 chops.

batali on brining

I brine just about anything that isn't going to be cooked for a long time. The reason I brine is because the salt in the water seasons the meat really deeply, plus the technique keeps the meat nice and succulent.

**For this recipe I like
to use Gaeta, Niçoise or
Moroccan dry-cured
olives. You want an
aggressively flavored
olive, not a delicate one.**

4. Add the peppers, onions, olives, red pepper flakes, and capers and stir with a wooden spoon to loosen the brown bits from the bottom of the pan. Add the wine and bring to a boil. Lower the heat, place the pork chops in the pepper mixture, and simmer for 10 minutes (the pork should be cooked to 135°F).

5. Season the sauce with salt and pepper to taste. Stir in the reserved onion tops, and serve.

BRINING Brining was originally used as a means of preserving meats and other foods. Since the advent of refrigeration, such preserving techniques have become unnecessary.

But brining has become popular again as a means of increasing the succulence of meat or bird cuts that lack fat or great flavor. Just enough salt is used to help the food retain its moisture content, and other flavors may be added with cider, beer, wine, various vinegars or other liquids, and sometimes, spices.

For a basic brine recipe, use 1 cup salt for each gallon of liquid. For each cup of salt used, boil 2 cups of water. Add the salt, and any spices and/or sugar, to the boiling water and stir to dissolve. Then add the remaining cold liquid to chill the brine and pour the liquid into a container deep enough to submerge the meat or poultry entirely. Place the meat or bird in the *cool* brine and, if necessary, weight down with a plate to keep it submerged. Refrigerate or place in a suitably cool place. Generally I like to keep it there overnight, but not a full 24 hours. Rinse the meat or fowl twice before cooking, and discard the brine.

Big Turkey Meatballs

Polpette di Tacchino

MAKES 6 SERVINGS

 8 to 10 thick slices day-old bread, cut into 1-inch cubes (4 cups)

 2 pounds ground turkey

 4 ounces prosciutto di Parma, cut into ⅛-inch dice

 8 ounces sweet Italian sausage, casings removed

 3 large eggs, lightly beaten

½ cup freshly grated Pecorino Romano

¼ cup freshly grated Parmigiano-Reggiano

¾ cup finely chopped Italian parsley

Several gratings of nutmeg

½ cup extra-virgin olive oil

Salt and freshly ground black pepper

 2 cups Basic Tomato Sauce (page 25)

½ cup dry white wine

1. Soak the bread in water to cover for 5 minutes. Squeeze out the excess water.

2. In a large bowl, combine the turkey, prosciutto, sausage, bread, eggs, ¼ cup of the pecorino, the Parmigiano, ½ cup of the parsley, the nutmeg, and ¼ cup of the olive oil and mix very gently with your hands. Season with salt and pepper. Form the mixture into 3-inch balls. Place the balls on a baking sheet, cover, and refrigerate for 1 hour to allow the flavors to blend.

3. In a 10- to 12-inch heavy-bottomed sauté pan, heat the remaining ¼ cup olive oil over high heat until almost smoking. Add the meatballs and brown on all sides. Transfer the meatballs to a plate and drain off the oil.

4. Add the tomato sauce and wine to the pan and bring to a boil. Place the meatballs in the sauce and return to a boil, then lower the heat and simmer for 30 minutes.

5. Transfer to a platter and serve with the remaining ¼ cup each pecorino and parsley sprinkled over the top.

Snapper with Olives

Cernia alle Olive

editor's note

Batali has a favored technique for segmenting citrus: Cut off the top and bottom of the fruit to slightly expose the flesh. Stand the fruit on a work surface; carefully cut off the skin and all the bitter white pith. To release the segments, hold the fruit over a bowl (to catch any juices) and cut down along either side of the membrane to free each section of the fruit.

A magnificent American delicacy, a real red snapper from the Gulf is one of the few American fish, along with wild striped bass and king salmon, that incite Italians to crazy jealousy when they eat here. The simplest method of cooking is always preferable with a fish as delicate as a snapper.

MAKES 4 SERVINGS

One 3- to 4-pound red snapper, cleaned and scaled
Flour for dredging
6 tablespoons extra-virgin olive oil
1 cup Gaeta olives, pitted and coarsely chopped
3 tablespoons salt-packed capers, rinsed
5 lemons, zested and segmented (see Editor's Note, at left)
Juice of 3 lemons
1 cup dry white wine
About ¼ cup best-quality extra-virgin olive oil
¼ cup finely chopped Italian parsley
Coarse sea salt

1. Preheat the oven to 450°F.

2. With a sharp knife, score the snapper twice on each side. Dredge the fish in the flour. In a 14-inch ovenproof sauté pan or a flameproof roasting pan, heat the 6 tablespoons olive oil over medium-high heat until just smoking. Place the fish in the pan and cook until golden brown on the first side. Carefully turn the fish and add the olives, capers, lemon zest, segments, and juice, and wine.

3. Place the pan in the oven and roast for 14 to 15 minutes, until the fish is just cooked through. Allow the fish to rest for 5 minutes.

4. To serve, fillet the fish, cut each fillet in half, and arrange on four plates. Drizzle with the pan juices and the ¼ cup best-quality olive oil, sprinkle with the parsley and salt, and serve.

BEST OF THE BEST EXCLUSIVE
Spaghetti with Crab and Jalapeños

6 SERVINGS

3	tablespoons unsalted butter
¼	cup plus 2 tablespoons extra-virgin olive oil
6	garlic cloves, thinly sliced
3	jalapeños, seeded and finely diced
½	cup dry white wine
1	pound jumbo lump crabmeat, picked over
1	pound spaghetti

Kosher salt and freshly ground pepper

1. Bring a large pot of salted water to a boil. In a very large deep skillet, melt the butter in ¼ cup of the olive oil. Add the garlic and cook over moderate heat until light golden, about 3 minutes. Add the jalapeños and cook for 1 minute. Add the wine, bring to a boil and remove from the heat. Gently stir in the crab, breaking up some of the larger pieces.

2. Add the spaghetti to the boiling water and cook until al dente. Drain well, reserving ½ cup of the pasta cooking liquid. Add the spaghetti to the skillet, then stir in the reserved pasta cooking liquid and the remaining 2 tablespoons of olive oil. Cook, over moderate heat, tossing, until the sauce coats the spaghetti. Season with salt and pepper, transfer to a bowl and serve.

editor's note

This recipe comes from the menu of Mario Batali's latest New York restaurant, Del Posto. Batali likes to use Dungeness crab at the restaurant, but jumbo lump crabmeat is a great substitute. If you want to make this dish on a budget, then any grade of fresh (not tinned) crab will work.

Rick Bayless grilling in his living room fireplace.

Mexican Everyday

by Rick Bayless with Deann Groen Bayless

Famed Chicago chef and prolific cookbook author Rick Bayless is known for intricate, authentic Mexican dishes. But in *Mexican Everyday,* his sixth book, he applies all his expertise to creating extremely tasty recipes that can be ready in half an hour—which makes them terrific for everyday cooking. These dishes are also nutritionally balanced, emphasizing lean protein, vegetables and grains. Bayless's love of spices and chiles, handled with a deft touch, comes through in every chapter.

Published by W. W. Norton, 336 pages, $29.95.

BEST RECIPES

Green Chile Chicken
Soft Tacos
36

Jícama Salad with
Watercress, Romaine and
Lime-Cilantro Dressing
41

Tomatillo Pork Braise with
Pickled Chiles
42

Jalapeño-Baked Fish
with Roasted Tomatoes
and Potatoes
45

**BEST OF THE BEST
EXCLUSIVE**

Melted Cheese Dip
with Tequila
47

Find more recipes by
Rick Bayless at
foodandwine.com/bayless

Green Chile Chicken Soft Tacos
Tacos de Pollo al Chile Poblano

editor's note

To reheat tortillas in the microwave, Bayless suggests this technique. Sprinkle 3 tablespoons water over a clean kitchen towel, then wrap the tortillas in it. Slip the wrapped tortillas into a microwaveable plastic bag and fold the top over, making sure not to seal it. Microwave at 50 percent power for 4 minutes. Let stand for 2 or 3 minutes before serving.

It may surprise you that until recently, delicious little soft tacos of seared chicken and roasted peppers didn't play much of a role in Mexico's *taquerías*. Boneless breasts from the good-size free-range chickens that country is known for just don't benefit from quick griddle-searing or grilling. But now that a good number of the toothsome barnyard chickens have been replaced by smaller, tenderer birds, chicken tacos are giving the classic beef ones a run for their money. It doesn't hurt that folks see them as a healthy alternative—without any sacrifice of flavor.

SERVES 4

  2 large fresh poblano chiles
  2 tablespoons vegetable or olive oil (divided use)
  1 large white onion, sliced ¼ inch thick
Salt
  1 pound (3 medium-large halves) boneless, skinless chicken breast halves
Ground black pepper
  3 tablespoons fresh lime juice
  2 garlic cloves, peeled and finely chopped or crushed through a garlic press
12 warm corn tortillas, store-bought (see Editor's Note, at left) or homemade
About ¾ cup Roasted Tomatillo Salsa (recipe follows) or Guacamole (recipe follows), or bottled salsa or hot sauce, for serving

Roast the poblanos over an open flame or 4 inches below a broiler, turning regularly until blistered and blackened all over, about 5 minutes for an open flame, 10 minutes for the broiler. Place in a bowl, cover with a kitchen towel and let cool until handleable.

Turn on (or adjust) the oven to its lowest setting. Heat 1 tablespoon of the oil in a very large (12-inch) skillet over medium-high. Add the onion and cook, stirring frequently, until golden but still crunchy, 4 to 5 minutes. Scoop into a heatproof serving bowl, leaving as much oil as possible in the skillet, and slide it into the oven. Set the skillet aside.

Rub the blackened skin off the chiles and pull out the stems and seed pods. Rinse the chiles to remove bits of skin and seeds. Cut into ¼-inch strips and stir into the onions. Taste and season with salt, usually a generous 1 teaspoon. Return the bowl to the oven.

Sprinkle both sides of the chicken breasts generously with salt and pepper.

Return the skillet to medium heat. Add the remaining 1 tablespoon oil. When the oil is hot, lay in the chicken breasts. Brown on one side, about 5 minutes, then flip and finish cooking on the other side, about 4 minutes more. When the meat is done, add the lime juice and garlic to the skillet. Turn the chicken in the lime mixture for a minute or so, until the juice has reduced to a glaze and coats the chicken.

Cut the chicken breasts into ¼-inch strips and toss with the onion-poblano mixture. Taste and season with additional salt if you think necessary. Serve with the warm tortillas and salsa, guacamole or hot sauce for making soft tacos.

A COUPLE OF RIFFS ON CHICKEN TACOS Grilling the chicken breasts is a delicious alternative to pan-searing them, but you'll miss the lime-garlic glaze. To solve that problem, I suggest you add the lime juice and garlic to the onions when they're browned, cooking until the liquid has reduced to a glaze. (You may want to have a little extra lime and garlic for marinating the chicken breasts before grilling.) If chicken tenders are more easily available than the breasts, use them; cooking time will be shorter. Beef skirt or flank steak works well here, too. And, of course, any of the large fleshy chiles (from Anaheims to red bell peppers) can stand in for the poblanos.

bayless on sour cream

I've never seen anyone ever use sour cream on tacos in Mexico! But if you think it tastes good, then go ahead— it's just more of an American thing.

Roasted Tomatillo Salsa
Salsa de Tomate Verde Asado

MAKES 1½ CUPS

2 large garlic cloves, peeled

4 medium (about 8 ounces total) tomatillos, husked, rinsed and halved

Hot green chiles to taste (I like 2 serranos or 1 jalapeño), stemmed and roughly chopped

About ⅓ cup (loosely packed) roughly chopped cilantro

½ small white onion, finely chopped

Salt

Set a large (10-inch) nonstick skillet over medium-high heat (if you don't have a nonstick skillet, lay in a piece of foil). Lay in the garlic and tomatillos, cut side down. When the tomatillos are well browned, 3 or 4 minutes, turn everything over and brown the other side. (The tomatillos should be completely soft.)

Scrape the tomatillos and garlic into a blender or food processor and let cool to room temperature, about 3 minutes. Add the chiles, cilantro and ¼ cup water. Blend to a coarse puree. Pour into a salsa dish and thin with a little additional water if necessary to give the salsa an easily spoonable consistency.

Scoop the chopped onion into a strainer and rinse under cold water. Stir into the salsa. Taste and season with salt, usually about ½ teaspoon.

RIFFS ON ROASTED TOMATILLO SALSA Though it's common and easy to use small hot green chiles in this salsa, one of my favorite versions includes a whole roasted, peeled and seeded poblano chile, coarsely pureed with the other ingredients. It may sound like heresy to Mexican cooks, but a dash of Worcestershire, balsamic vinegar or coarse-grain mustard is good in this salsa. If I'm serving the salsa with something off the grill, I'll slow-grill a large green onion or two (or just a slice of white onion), chop it and add it in place of the raw onion. To underscore the tomatillo's natural citrusy tang, I sometimes add a little fresh lime juice. Or go full-bore fruity and stir in finely chopped pineapple, apple or pear.

PASTA WITH ROASTED TOMATILLOS AND CHICKEN OR SALMON Put on a pot of water to boil, then make the salsa, without letting the ingredients cool. Boil 12 ounces pasta (fusilli or shells are good choices) in salted water until al dente. Drain, reserving ¼ cup of the cooking liquid. Return the pasta to the pot, and add the salsa, the reserved cooking liquid and 2 cups coarsely shredded cooked chicken or salmon—I usually buy rotisserie chicken or pepper-coated hot-smoked salmon that's easy to flake. Sprinkle on a generous cup grated Mexican *queso añejo* or Parmesan, toss and serve with chopped cilantro, extra cheese and a few wedges of lime for each hungry eater to add to his or her liking. Wonderful at room temperature for a picnic.

Guacamole Three Ways: Simple, Herby or Luxurious

Guacamole Tres Estilos

MAKES 1¼ TO 1½ CUPS

2 medium ripe avocados

1 garlic clove, peeled and finely chopped or crushed through a garlic press

Salt

To make it herby, add:

2 tablespoons chopped cilantro

About 1 tablespoon fresh lime juice

To make it luxurious, also add:

Fresh hot green chile to taste (I like 1 serrano or ½ to 1 jalapeño), finely chopped

¼ small white onion, finely chopped

½ medium tomato, chopped into ¼-inch dice

Cut the avocados in half, running your knife around the pit from stem to blossom end and back up again. Twist the halves in opposite directions to free the pit, and pull the halves apart. Dislodge the pit, then scoop the avocado flesh into a medium bowl.

bayless's favorite hot sauce

I like the brand Tamazula from Mexico. It's my very favorite—especially the extra-hot, which is richer in flavor.

Mash the avocado with a large fork or potato masher. Stir in the garlic and about ½ teaspoon salt, plus any other sets of ingredients you've chosen. If your list includes white onion, rinse it first under cold water, then shake well to rid it of excess moisture before adding to the avocado. (This reduces the risk of having the onion flavor overwhelm the guacamole.) Taste and season with additional salt if appropriate. If not using immediately, cover with plastic wrap pressed directly on the surface of the guacamole and refrigerate—preferably for no more than a few hours.

A RIFF ON "STAGE TWO" GUACAMOLE Replace the lime juice with (or, for extra-tangy guacamole, add along with the lime juice) about ½ cup bottled tomatillo salsa—perfect as a topping or a dip, especially when you need to make the guacamole ahead (the additional acid from the tomatillos helps keep the guacamole greener for longer).

AVOCADO SAUCE For a tangy sauce to drizzle over raw (or blanched) vegetables or on tacos, tostadas and the like, follow the above variation, increasing the tomatillo salsa to 1 cup; puree everything in a blender. If the sauce is too thick to drizzle, thin with additional tomatillo salsa. A little heavy cream, sour cream or *crème fraîche* can be added for wonderful richness.

MY TWENTY-FIFTH WEDDING ANNIVERSARY BREAKFAST I resurrected this forgotten recipe that I had created the year Deann and I got married. Shred 2 medium-large (10 to 12 ounces total) red-skin boiling or Yukon Gold potatoes; squeeze out excess moisture between your hands. Heat a very large (12-inch) skillet over medium and lightly coat with oil. Form 4 small potato pancakes, sprinkle with salt and press flat with a spatula. When browned on one side, flip and brown the other side. Smear with the simplest guacamole, top each with a poached egg and sprinkle with salt, black pepper and chopped cilantro.

Jícama Salad with Watercress, Romaine and Lime-Cilantro Dressing

Ensalada de Jícama con Berros, Cilantro, Lechuga Orejona y Limón

Mexican Everyday

RICK BAYLESS WITH
DEANN GROEN BAYLESS

SERVES 4

¾ cup vegetable oil, olive oil or a mixture of the two

⅓ cup fresh lime juice

½ teaspoon grated lime zest (colored rind only)

½ cup (packed) roughly chopped cilantro

Fresh hot green chiles to taste (I like 2 serranos or 1 jalapeño), stemmed and roughly chopped (optional)

Salt

1 medium (about 1 pound) firm, unblemished jícama, peeled and cut into sticks (¼ inch is a good width, 2 inches a good length)

1 medium bunch watercress, large lower stems broken off (about 2 cups)

4 good-size romaine leaves, cut crosswise in ¼-inch slices (about 2 cups)

Combine the oil, lime juice, lime zest, cilantro, chiles and a scant teaspoon salt in a blender jar. Blend until smooth. Pour into a jar and secure the lid.

In a large bowl, combine the jícama, watercress and romaine. Shake the dressing to combine thoroughly, then drizzle on about ¼ cup. (Cover and refrigerate the remaining dressing for another salad.) Toss to combine. Taste and season with a little more salt if you think necessary. Serve right away.

RIFFS ON JÍCAMA SALAD Arugula or mâche could replace the watercress, while cucumber could replace part of the jícama. A few toasted pine nuts are delicious sprinkled over the salad. If you're partial to fruit, add some diced mango. A little crumbled Mexican *queso fresco* or goat cheese is really, really good on the fruit version of the salad.

editor's note

Bayless says that the best way to peel jícama is with a knife rather than a vegetable peeler. That way, you'll cut a little deeper and slice away the tough, fibrous layer just below the skin.

Tomatillo Pork Braise with Pickled Chiles

Puerco en Salsa Verde con Jalapeños Encurtidos

I know that the idea of rich, meaty pork braised with tangy tomatillos, garlic and herbs may ring a bell for many of you, since a related (but more involved, more special-occasion) dish from my *Mexico One Plate at a Time* has become a favorite at dinner tables all across our country. It demands a sequel, because this version illustrates how a slow-cooker (plus a dash of Worcestershire) can be invaluable in the creation of deep, roasty flavors that would otherwise require the time-consuming roasting of individual sauce ingredients. This homier version of the dressier classic is perfect enjoyed in big bowls around the fireplace in the winter, or, without the beans, as a filling for soft tacos. It's a good buffet dish, too.

SERVES 6

1½ pounds (10 to 12 medium) tomatillos, husked, rinsed and cut into 1-inch pieces

3 garlic cloves, peeled and halved

3 to 4 canned pickled jalapeños, stemmed, halved and seeds scraped out

½ cup (loosely packed) roughly chopped cilantro (divided use)

Salt

1½ to 2 pounds boneless pork shoulder, cut into 1-inch cubes

1 tablespoon Worcestershire sauce

Two 15-ounce cans large white (Great Northern or cannellini) beans, drained

About ½ teaspoon sugar, if needed

Scoop the tomatillos into a slow-cooker and spread them in an even layer. Scatter on the garlic, jalapeños and half of the cilantro. Sprinkle evenly with 1½ teaspoons salt.

In a large bowl, combine the pork and Worcestershire, mixing until the cubes are well coated. Distribute the meat over the tomatillo mixture. Cover and slow-cook on high for 6 hours (the dish can hold on the slow-cooker's "keep warm" function for 4 more hours or so).

With a pair of tongs, remove the pork to a bowl. Tip or ladle the sauce mixture into a blender and add the remaining cilantro. Cover loosely and blend until smooth; return the mixture to the slow-cooker. (Alternatively, you can puree the sauce in the slow-cooker using an immersion blender.) Stir in the drained beans. Taste and season with salt if necessary; stir in a little water if the sauce has thickened beyond the consistency of a light cream soup. Add a little sugar if the sauce is too tart for you. Return the meat to the pot, let everything warm through and you're ready to serve.

NO SLOW-COOKER? In a medium-large (4- to 6-quart; 10- to 12-inch-diameter) heavy pot, preferably a Dutch oven, layer the tomatillos, flavorings and meat as described. Cover with the sauce, set the lid in place and braise in a 300-degree oven for 2½ to 3 hours, until the pork is completely tender. Complete the dish as described.

RIFFS ON PORK IN TOMATILLO SAUCE If beans don't appeal to you, replace them with potatoes or small sweet turnips (cut into wedges) or carrots (2-inch lengths cut into sticks). Toss them with a little salt and place them on top of the sauce ingredients (tomatillos, garlic and chile) before layering in the pork. Take them out with the meat while you finish the sauce. I also like to add a big handful of spinach to the blender when pureeing the sauce; a few tablespoons of Mexican *crema, crème fraîche* or heavy cream work magic on this spinach-enhanced sauce. *Epazote* is a favorite replacement for cilantro in many parts of Mexico; *hoja santa* is a personal favorite, but I don't add it until I'm blending the sauce. The pickled jalapeños take the sauce in a delicious direction, but you could use poblanos: roast, peel and seed 2 poblanos and add them to the blender when pureeing the sauce.

As you might expect, this dish is perfectly delicious made with 2 pounds boneless, skinless chicken thighs. If you're a lamb or beef lover, replace the pork shoulder with 1-inch pieces of boneless lamb shoulder or beef chuck; double the cilantro (the lamb and beef need the extra punch) and use 2 poblanos, as described just above. Both lamb and beef benefit greatly from browning before slow-cooking.

Jalapeño-Baked Fish with Roasted Tomatoes and Potatoes

Pescado Horneado al Jalapeño

This is one of the simplest, tastiest, come-back-to-it-often dishes I know. It can be made even simpler if you replace the tomato mixture with 2 cups of bottled tomato salsa. I'd be hard-pressed to say where they make a dish like this in Mexico, especially since baked dishes aren't a part of the traditional, mostly stovetop cuisine. But the idea of fish cooked in roasted tomato sauce sparked with jalapeño chiles and cilantro is about as traditional as you can get. Even the potatoes make a regular showing in dishes like this. If, like me, you weave lots of vegetables into your everyday eating, feel free to sprinkle the dish with steamed peas before spooning on the sauce.

SERVES 4

- 4 medium (1 pound total) red-skin boiling or Yukon Gold potatoes, sliced ¼ inch thick
- 1 tablespoon vegetable or olive oil

Salt

One 15-ounce can diced tomatoes in juice (preferably fire-roasted)

- 1 large garlic clove, peeled and cut in half
- ⅓ cup (loosely packed) coarsely chopped cilantro, plus extra for garnish

About ¼ cup sliced canned pickled jalapeños (you can seed and slice whole pickled jalapeños or buy "nacho slices")

- 1 tablespoon jalapeño pickling juice

Four 4- to 5-ounce (1 to 1¼ pounds total) skinless fish fillets (mahimahi, halibut, black cod and striped bass are all good here), preferably ¾ to 1 inch thick

Turn on the oven to 400 degrees. Scoop the sliced potatoes into a microwaveable 8 x 8-inch baking dish. Drizzle on the oil and sprinkle with ½ teaspoon salt. Toss to coat, then spread the potatoes in an even layer. Cover with plastic wrap and poke a couple of holes in the top. Microwave on high (100%) until the potatoes are nearly tender, about 4 to 5 minutes.

Meanwhile, in a food processor or blender, combine the tomatoes with their juice, garlic, cilantro, jalapeños and pickling juice. Process to a puree, leaving just a little texture.

bayless on 10-minute meals

If I'm pressed for time, I make chilaquiles. I fry up some garlic in olive oil with a minced chipotle packed in adobo. I add a tin of Muir Glen fire-roasted tomatoes to make a soupy sauce. Then I add corn tortillas to the sauce and wait until they're soft. It comes out like a saucy pasta dish. I serve it topped with shredded meat or grated cheese and some cilantro.

Lay the fish fillets in a single layer over the potatoes. Pour the tomato mixture evenly over the fish and potatoes.

Slide the baking dish into the oven. Bake for 15 to 20 minutes, until the fish flakes when pressed firmly.

Scoop a portion of fish, potatoes and sauce onto each dinner plate, sprinkle with cilantro and serve right away.

RIFFS ON JALAPEÑO-BAKED FISH This is a wonderful place to feature the Mexican white-fleshed sweet potato (*camote morado*), yuca or other roots from Caribbean groceries. All of them have pretty fibrous exteriors, so trim them, slice them and microwave them with a good sprinkling of water (they are naturally drier than potatoes) and salt. Be prepared for them to take a little longer than potatoes to cook.

Herbs like Mexican oregano, thyme and marjoram make a delicious addition to the sauce, as do a handful of golden (or regular) raisins. You can go all the way to the classic Veracruzana flavors by adding some chopped olives and capers. A delicious alternative to the basic recipe replaces the tomato mixture with 2 cups tomatillo salsa (store-bought or the Roasted Tomatillo Salsa on page 38). That version is wonderful too when you substitute sliced baby artichokes (peel off the tough outer leaves first, trim the fibrous exterior off the base and slice ¼ inch thick) for half the potatoes—microwave the artichokes with the potatoes.

BEST OF THE BEST EXCLUSIVE

Melted Cheese Dip with Tequila

Queso Fundido al Tequila

6 SERVINGS

- 1 tablespoon extra-virgin olive oil
- 2 medium tomatoes—cored, seeded and cut into ¼-inch dice (1¼ cups)
- 2 medium jalapeños, seeded and minced
- 1 small onion, cut into ¼-inch dice

Kosher salt

- 3 tablespoons tequila
- ½ pound Monterey Jack cheese, shredded (3 cups)
- ¼ cup chopped cilantro

Warm corn tortillas or corn chips, for serving

1. In a large skillet, heat the olive oil. Add the tomatoes, jalapeños, onion and a large pinch of salt and cook over moderately high heat, stirring often, until softened, about 5 minutes. Add the tequila and cook, stirring frequently, until the pan looks dry, about 2 minutes.

2. Reduce the heat to low. Add the cheese and cook, stirring constantly, until fully melted, about 30 seconds. Quickly transfer the cheese dip to a serving bowl. Sprinkle with the cilantro and serve immediately with tortillas or chips.

editor's note

Bayless really likes to use an authentic Mexican melting cheese like Chihuahua (Supremo is his preferred brand) in place of the Monterey Jack in this dish (available from 1800gourmet.com).

Luisa Osborne's Shrimp
Pancakes, p. 50

La Cocina de Mamá

by Penelope Casas

"Even Spain's greatest chefs, in their leisure time, prefer the dishes passed down to them by their *mamás*," declares Spanish food expert Penelope Casas. In her sixth book, *La Cocina de Mamá*, Casas focuses on the lifeblood of Spanish cuisine—the simple recipes of home cooks. Casas carefully describes each dish, providing a little Spanish history and local flavor along with recipes like Moorish-Style Green Salad with Cumin and Paprika, and Chicken and Sparerib Stew.

Published by Broadway Books, 320 pages, $29.95.

BEST RECIPES

Luisa Osborne's
Shrimp Pancakes
50

Moorish-Style Green
Salad with Cumin
and Paprika
51

Chicken and
Sparerib Stew
52

**BEST OF THE BEST
EXCLUSIVE**

Shrimp and Avocado
Phyllo Triangles
55

Find more recipes by
Penelope Casas at
foodandwine.com/casas

Luisa Osborne's Shrimp Pancakes

Tortitas de Camarones de Luisa Osborne

editor's note

Smoked paprika (*pimentón*) is an essential ingredient in Spanish cooking— for stews, paellas and grilled meats. Casas says that smoked paprika from Extremadura is especially prized for its pronounced earthy flavor and can range from sweet (*dulce*) to bittersweet (*agridulce*) to hot (*picante*).

This recipe includes the shrimp shells, which give additional shrimp flavor and extra crispness to the pancakes.

MAKES 20 PANCAKES

Kosher or sea salt
¼ pound very small shrimp in their shells
2 tablespoons minced onion
1 garlic clove, minced
2 tablespoons minced fresh parsley
⅛ teaspoon sweet paprika, preferably Spanish smoked (see Editor's Note, at left)
½ cup flour
Mild olive oil for frying

Bring to a boil in a small saucepan about 1 cup water with ½ teaspoon salt. Add the shrimp and cook briefly until just opaque. Remove with a slotted spoon and measure the liquid to ½ cup plus 2 tablespoons (boil down if there is more). Transfer the liquid to a bowl and cool.

Chop the shrimp with their shells into approximately ⅛-inch pieces. Add to the cooled liquid with the onion, garlic, parsley, paprika, flour, and salt to taste and stir until smooth. Let sit for 1 hour at room temperature. The mixture should have the consistency of a thin pancake batter.

Pour the oil to a depth of ¼ inch into a large skillet and heat to the smoking point. Drop the batter by the tablespoon into the oil, spreading and pricking with the edge of a spoon into thin, lacy-textured pancakes. Fry until golden, then flip them over to brown the other side. Drain on paper towels. Keep warm in a 200°F oven while preparing the rest of the pancakes. Transfer to a platter and serve.

Moorish-Style Green Salad with Cumin and Paprika

Ensalada Mora

Cumin and paprika are two wonderful additions to a salad dressing, an idea that comes from southern Spain. It is excellent on any green or mixed salad.

SERVES 4

- ¾ teaspoon cumin seeds or ground cumin
- 1 large garlic clove, minced
- ½ teaspoon sweet paprika, preferably Spanish smoked (see Editor's Note, at left)
- 1 tablespoon minced fresh parsley

Kosher or sea salt

- 4 teaspoons red or white wine vinegar
- 3 tablespoons plus 1 teaspoon extra virgin olive oil

About 4 cups tender torn romaine or escarole leaves, or mesclun

In a mortar mash the cumin, garlic, paprika, parsley, and ⅛ teaspoon salt. Whisk in the vinegar and the oil and add salt to taste.

Place the greens in a salad bowl and toss in the dressing to serve.

Chicken and Sparerib Stew

Guiso Caldoso de Aldea Antiguo

casas on preparing spareribs

This recipe calls for the spareribs to be hacked into two-inch pieces. I've done it at home, but you have to have a huge knife and you really have to do a lot of hard work. So it's best if you have the butcher do it for you.

A magnificent dish from our friend Digna Prieto, a veritable ball of energy despite her advanced years. This, she tells me, is an old village recipe from Galicia, and it filled my kitchen with the wonderful aromas that greet you at lunchtime in little villages all over Spain. The additions of saffron and cumin give the stew a haunting flavor. A green salad is all you need to complete this meal.

SERVES 5 TO 6

- 2 tablespoons olive oil
- 1 pound pork spareribs or baby back ribs, hacked into 2-inch pieces, fat trimmed

Kosher or sea salt

Freshly ground pepper

- ¾ cup chicken broth

One 3- to 3½-pound chicken

About ¼ pound pancetta, cut into ¾-inch slices, then into ¾-inch cubes

- 1 medium carrot, peeled and finely chopped
- 4 garlic cloves, minced
- 1 medium onion, finely chopped
- 4 tablespoons minced fresh parsley
- ½ pound small new potatoes, about 2 inches in diameter, peeled and cut in halves
- ½ cup fresh or frozen peas
- ¼ teaspoon cumin, preferably freshly ground
- ⅛ teaspoon crumbled thread saffron

In a shallow casserole, heat 1 tablespoon of the oil and sauté the pork ribs until browned, sprinkling with salt and pepper as they cook. Stir in the broth and ⅓ cup water. Bring to a boil, cover, and simmer for 1 hour (this can be done in advance). Meanwhile, cut the chicken into small serving pieces. Detach the wings and legs, hack off the bony ends of the legs, cut off and discard the wing tips, and divide each wing into 2 parts. With kitchen shears, divide the breast and each thigh into 4 pieces. Sprinkle with salt and let sit at room temperature.

Remove the ribs to a warm platter and measure the broth to 1½ cups, adding water if there is less. Skim off the fat that rises to the surface. Reserve the ribs and broth and wipe out the casserole. Heat the remaining tablespoon oil in the casserole and brown the chicken and pancetta, turning once. Add the carrot, garlic, onion, and parsley and sauté until the vegetables are softened.

Add the reserved ribs and broth and the potatoes to the casserole. Bring to a boil, cover, and simmer for 25 minutes. Stir in the peas, cumin, saffron, and salt and pepper to taste. Cover and continue cooking for 15 minutes more. Serve.

BEST OF THE BEST EXCLUSIVE

Shrimp and Avocado Phyllo Triangles

Bric de Verduras, Langostinos y Aguacate

MAKES SIXTEEN 3-INCH PASTRIES

- 2 tablespoons extra-virgin olive oil, plus more for frying
- 1 large carrot, finely julienned
- 1 large leek, white part only, finely julienned
- ¼ pound large shrimp—shelled, deveined and finely chopped
- ½ Haas avocado, cut into ⅓-inch dice

Kosher salt and freshly ground pepper

Four 12-by-17-inch sheets of phyllo dough

editor's note

Although this recipe calls for the phyllo triangles to be deep-fried, they can also be baked: Brush them generously with olive oil and bake for 35 minutes at 350°.

1. In a medium skillet, heat the 2 tablespoons of olive oil. Add the carrot and leek and cook over moderately low heat until tender, about 7 minutes. Increase the heat to moderate, add the shrimp and cook until just opaque, about 2 minutes. Transfer the shrimp and vegetables to a bowl and let cool. Gently mix in the avocado and season with salt and pepper.

2. Stack the phyllo sheets on a work surface and cut them crosswise into 4 strips, each about 4 by 12 inches. Arrange the strips of one stack on a work surface with the short ends facing you; keep the remaining phyllo covered with a damp towel to prevent it from drying out. Spoon a heaping tablespoon of the shrimp filling in one corner of each strip; fold the corner over the filling to form a triangle. Continue folding the phyllo up and over onto itself as you would fold a flag, sealing the final folds with water. Transfer the phyllo triangles to a plate. Repeat with the remaining phyllo and filling.

3. In a large, deep skillet, heat ⅓ inch of olive oil until it reaches 360°. Fry the triangles over moderate heat, turning once, until golden brown on both sides, about 2 minutes total. Drain on paper towels and serve hot.

Spicy Linguine with Sautéed
Baby Squid and Chorizo, p. 58

Chef, Interrupted

by Melissa Clark

"The hardest thing about writing this book was getting the chefs to send me their recipes," declares Melissa Clark. "I had to threaten, I had to beg and plead, I had to do whatever it took!" In *Chef, Interrupted,* Clark's 17th cookbook, she's collected dishes from more than 50 of the nation's most acclaimed chefs. She's then pared them down for the home cook by substituting hard-to-find ingredients with more accessible ones and complex techniques with more basic approaches. The results do the chefs proud—and Clark, too.

Published by Clarkson Potter, 272 pages, $32.50.

BEST RECIPES

Spicy Linguine with Sautéed Baby Squid and Chorizo
58

Braised Basque Chicken with Tomatoes and Paprika
60

Rack of Lamb with a Cumin and Salt Crust, Lemon, and Cilantro
62

BEST OF THE BEST EXCLUSIVE

Shredded Brussels Sprouts Salad with Walnuts and Manchego
65

Find more recipes by Melissa Clark at **foodandwine.com/clark**

Spicy Linguine with Sautéed Baby Squid and Chorizo

editor's note

Chorizo is a Spanish pork sausage spiced with smoked paprika. Clark recommends seeking out chorizo that is well marbled with fat as it will have a better flavor and crisp up nicely in the pan. You can order this, and other Spanish products, from La Tienda (888-472-1022 or tienda.com).

This dish is as much about the squid as it is about the pasta. The idea of combining squid, chorizo, and pasta came from Eric Ripert's gorgeous book, *A Return to Cooking.* His recipe uses cuttlefish, a relative of squid, and is naturally a lot more complex than my adaptation.

SERVES 4 AS A MAIN COURSE, 8 AS A SMALL PASTA COURSE OR APPETIZER

Coarse sea salt or kosher salt

½ pound linguine

4 tablespoons extra-virgin olive oil

1¼ cups (about 4 ounces) thinly sliced Spanish chorizo (see Editor's Note, at left)

3 garlic cloves

¼ teaspoon hot paprika (see Editor's Note, page 60)

1 pound squid, cut into rings (see Note that follows)

Freshly ground black pepper to taste

2 tablespoons freshly squeezed lemon juice (from 1 lemon)

2 tablespoons chopped fresh flat-leaf parsley, for garnish

1 tablespoon chopped fresh chives, for garnish

PREPARATION TIME: 30 MINUTES

1. Bring a large pot of salted water to a boil. Add the pasta and cook until just al dente. Drain and toss with 1 tablespoon of the oil to prevent sticking.

2. In a large skillet over low heat, warm the remaining 3 tablespoons of oil. Add the chorizo and cook it slowly until it has rendered its fat and begun to get crisp on the edges, about 6 minutes. Add the garlic and paprika along with a pinch of salt and sauté for 1 minute, taking care not to burn the garlic. Add the squid and cook for 2 more minutes, tossing well. Add the cooked linguine and toss to coat. Season generously with salt and pepper.

3. Just before serving, add the lemon juice, toss, and garnish with the fresh parsley and chives.

NOTE

Squid and calamari should smell fresh and saline and look gray on the outside. You can have your fishmonger clean the squid for you, or spend a few minutes doing it yourself. To clean squid, cut off the tentacles just below the eyes, pull out the hard beak, and rinse the tentacles well to remove any grit. Run the back of a large knife along the squid's body, scraping the innards out the open end. Pull or scrape off the remaining gray membrane from the bodies. Rinse well and slice the bodies and tentacles into rings.

Most squid you buy at the fishmonger's has already been frozen and thawed, so I usually get it still frozen and only thaw as much as I need at one time. It defrosts in a few minutes under cool running water.

clark on cooking chorizo

When you are cooking the chorizo, you only want enough fat in the pan to sauté the other ingredients. If there is too much, just spoon it off.

Braised Basque Chicken with Tomatoes and Paprika

Although I've known Daniel Boulud for years, he and I didn't really work together until I helped him write his cookbook *Global Braise* (Ecco Books, 2006). The books are but a small part of Daniel's empire, a well-oiled machine that includes the restaurants, television appearances, charity benefits, designing a line of pots and pans and a line of knives, the catering. Daniel can multitask like no one I know. I've seen him simultaneously talk on his cell phone to Japan, edit a recipe, and notice a sloppy bit of garnishing on the line from twelve feet above. For him, it's all about the details; he and I wrangled over them incessantly for the book—with me wanting to cut corners to make a recipe more home-cook friendly and him wincing at the prospect of, say, not covering a braised chicken dish with a round of parchment paper. Whenever I did win a point in the end, it's because he let me. For this recipe, well, since this is my book, he had no choice.

SERVES 6

4 ounces Spanish chorizo, sliced ¼ inch thick (see Editor's Note, page 58)

3 pounds chicken legs and thighs

Coarse sea salt or kosher salt and freshly ground black pepper

2 red bell peppers, stemmed, seeded, and cut into ½-inch-thick strips

2 small red onions, sliced

6 garlic cloves, thinly sliced

2 large sprigs of fresh thyme

¾ cup dry sherry

1 cup halved cherry tomatoes (or diced plum tomatoes)

2 teaspoons sweet paprika (see Editor's Note, at left)

¾ teaspoon crushed red pepper flakes, or to taste

Thinly sliced fresh basil leaves, for garnish

PREPARATION TIME: 40 MINUTES, PLUS 25 TO 30 MINUTES BRAISING

1. Preheat the oven to 350°F. In a large ovenproof sauté pan over medium heat, cook the chorizo on both sides until it begins to brown and render its fat, about 5 minutes. Use a slotted spoon to transfer the chorizo to a plate. Season the chicken well with salt and pepper, then brown the chicken pieces in the pan in two batches, for about 10 minutes per batch; transfer the browned chicken to plates lined with paper towels.

2. Pour off all but about 2 tablespoons of the fat from the pan. Add the bell peppers, onions, garlic, and thyme, season with salt, and sauté until soft, about 5 minutes. Add the sherry, tomatoes, paprika, and red pepper flakes and simmer for 1 minute, stirring to scrape up the browned bits from the bottom of the pan.

3. Return the chicken and chorizo to the pan, cover, and place in the oven until the chicken is cooked through, 25 to 30 minutes, turning the chicken occasionally. Adjust the seasoning, garnish with basil, and serve.

Rack of Lamb with a Cumin and Salt Crust, Lemon, and Cilantro

editor's note

This recipe calls for poaching a whole head of garlic in oil. Since you'll only need a couple of cloves for this recipe, Clark says to spread any extra on crostini or add it to salad dressing. It will keep in the refrigerator for up to a week.

Over the past twenty-five years that Chanterelle has been open, David Waltuck's cuisine has gone from pretty straight-ahead French-American to more global in scope, including influences from Asia and the Mediterranean. In this recipe for rack of lamb, he combines ingredients from them all, with the lemon and garlic sauce recalling Greece, the cilantro from Southeast Asia, and the rack of lamb from France. This twist on a classic offers flavors that are both familiar and compelling; it's the kind of dish you'll want to make over and over. And now that I've simplified it (eliminating a separate sauce and combining several steps), you can.

SERVES 4 TO 6

- 3 tablespoons ground cumin
- 1 tablespoon coarse sea salt or kosher salt, plus more to taste
- 2 teaspoons freshly ground black pepper, plus more to taste
- 2 racks of lamb (about 1¼ pounds each)
- 1 head of garlic, separated into cloves and peeled
- ½ cup plus 3 tablespoons extra-virgin olive oil
- ½ cup chicken broth, low-sodium if canned
- ¼ cup dry white wine
- 2 tablespoons freshly squeezed lemon juice (from 1 lemon)
- 3 tablespoons unsalted butter
- ¼ cup fresh cilantro leaves, for garnish

PREPARATION TIME: 1 HOUR AND 15 MINUTES, PLUS 30 MINUTES RESTING

1. Preheat the oven to 500°F and place a heavy-duty metal roasting pan in the oven to heat up.

2. In a bowl, combine the cumin, salt, and pepper. Rinse the lamb and shake it dry, but don't dry it completely—you want the seasoning to stick. Put the lamb on a plate and rub it all over with the cumin mixture. Let sit for about 20 minutes while the oven and pan preheat.

clark on schooling chefs
Some of the more savvy chefs know they're out of touch with the home cook. Some of them actually admitted to learning a few techniques from my book!

3. Meanwhile, put the garlic in a pan and cover with ½ cup of the olive oil. Bring the mixture to a bare simmer (there should be only a bubble or two) and let cook gently until the cloves are very soft, 20 to 30 minutes. Set aside.

4. When the roasting pan is very hot, carefully add the remaining 3 tablespoons of the olive oil (it may splatter) and place the lamb, fat side down, into the pan. Roast the lamb until nicely browned on the bottom, about 10 minutes, then flip the racks and cook about 5 minutes on the other side for rare (about 120°F on an instant-read thermometer), or cook it more or less to taste. If the fat side is not as brown as you would like at this point, turn the broiler to high and broil until really brown, 2 to 3 minutes longer. Transfer the lamb to a carving board and let rest for about 10 minutes.

5. Place the roasting pan on the stovetop over high heat. Add the chicken broth and use a wooden spoon to scrape up the browned bits from the bottom of the pan. Pass 2 of the roasted garlic cloves through a garlic press into the sauce, or smash them in a bowl and add the paste to the sauce. Add the wine and lemon juice and simmer until slightly thickened, about 6 minutes. Whisk in the butter and season with salt and pepper.

6. Serve the lamb with the pan sauce, garnished with cilantro leaves.

BEST OF THE BEST EXCLUSIVE

Shredded Brussels Sprouts Salad with Walnuts and Manchego

4 SERVINGS

- 1 cup walnut halves
- 10 ounces brussels sprouts, trimmed
- 2 tablespoons fresh lemon juice

Kosher salt

- 6 tablespoons extra-virgin olive oil
- ¾ cup (3 ounces) coarsely grated Manchego cheese

Freshly ground pepper

1. Preheat the oven to 350°. Spread the walnuts on a rimmed baking sheet and toast for 10 minutes, or until golden and fragrant. Transfer to a plate to cool, then coarsely chop the nuts.

2. In a food processor, finely shred the brussels sprouts. Transfer to a medium serving bowl. Toss the brussels sprouts with the lemon juice and 1 teaspoon of kosher salt, and let stand for 5 minutes. Add the toasted walnuts, olive oil and Manchego and toss. Season with salt and pepper and serve.

editor's note

Tossing fresh, crunchy shredded brussels sprouts with olive oil, cheese and nuts makes a perfect winter salad. It's a great (and original) way to prepare brussels sprouts— and the salad holds up well overnight in the refrigerator.

Verdure al Forno, p. 68

Everyday Italian

by Giada De Laurentiis

Few Italian *nonne* cook with canned chicken broth, pre-grated mozzarella or Pillsbury dough. But in her first cookbook, thirtysomething Food Network star Giada De Laurentiis isn't afraid to update old family recipes with these American convenience foods—and the results are impressive. Indeed, many of the recipes require just half a dozen ingredients and 30 minutes or less in the kitchen. The Roasted Pork Loin with Fig Sauce, for instance, is wonderfully juicy and delicious.

Published by Clarkson Potter, 256 pages, $30.

Find more recipes by
Giada De Laurentiis at
**foodandwine.com/
delaurentiis**

Verdure al Forno

Even though this dish uses only zucchini, my grandmother called it Verdure al Forno, which means "vegetables in the oven." (So it should really be called *Zucchine al Forno*, but there was absolutely no way anybody would tell that to my grandmother.) You could substitute eggplant, summer squash, potatoes, or even cauliflower for the zucchini and make this your very own Verdure al Forno.

4 SIDE-DISH SERVINGS

- 2 teaspoons extra-virgin olive oil
- 5 medium zucchini (about 1½ pounds total), cut crosswise into 1-inch-thick slices
- ½ teaspoon salt, plus more to taste
- ½ teaspoon freshly ground black pepper, plus more to taste
- 1 cup heavy cream
- 1 cup grated mozzarella cheese
- 1 cup grated fontina cheese
- 6 tablespoons grated Pecorino Romano cheese
- 1 cup plain dried bread crumbs

Preheat the oven to 350 degrees F. Line a baking sheet with foil. Coat the bottom of an 8-inch square baking dish with the oil. Arrange enough of the zucchini slices over the bottom of the dish in a single layer to cover. Sprinkle with one third of the salt and pepper. Pour ⅓ cup of the heavy cream over the zucchini and sprinkle with ⅓ cup each of mozzarella cheese and fontina cheese.

Sprinkle with 2 tablespoons of Pecorino Romano cheese, then with ⅓ cup of bread crumbs. Repeat layering the ingredients two more times. (The vegetables can be assembled 8 hours ahead. Cover and refrigerate. Bring to room temperature before proceeding.) Place the baking dish on the baking sheet and bake uncovered until golden brown on top and the sauce bubbles, about 40 minutes. Serve immediately.

Roasted Pork Loin with Fig Sauce

This dish is perfect for entertaining a large group because it serves a crowd and looks spectacular, and the rich, velvety fig sauce will knock your guests' socks off; it's so sweet you could even serve it over ice cream. Many European cultures have traditional recipes that pair pork with sweet fruit, usually apples. But apples aren't so prevalent in Italy, and figs are. Lucky for Italians.

4 TO 6 MAIN-COURSE SERVINGS

FIG SAUCE

2½ cups port

1¼ cups reduced-sodium chicken broth

  8 dried black Mission figs, coarsely chopped

  2 sprigs of fresh rosemary

  2 cinnamon sticks

  1 tablespoon honey

  2 tablespoons unsalted butter, cut into pieces

¼ teaspoon salt

¼ teaspoon freshly ground black pepper

PORK

  2 tablespoons olive oil

  2 tablespoons chopped fresh rosemary

  1 tablespoon salt, plus more to taste

1½ teaspoons freshly ground black pepper, plus more to taste

  1 4- to 4½-pound boneless pork loin

  1 cup low-sodium chicken broth

FOR THE FIG SAUCE

In a medium-size, heavy saucepan, combine the port, chicken broth, figs, rosemary, cinnamon, and honey. Boil over medium-high heat until reduced by half, about 30 minutes. Discard the rosemary sprigs and cinnamon sticks (some of the rosemary leaves will remain in the port mixture). Transfer the port mixture to a blender and purée until smooth. Blend in the butter, salt, and

de laurentiis's favorite sweet treats

I love Nutella and sometimes, when I need a pick-me-up, I just stick a teaspoon in the jar. I'm a dark chocolate fan, too; milk is fine, but it doesn't give me that kick. And white chocolate? Well, white just doesn't count.

pepper. (The sauce can be made 1 day ahead. Cover and refrigerate. Rewarm over medium heat before using.)

FOR THE PORK

Preheat the oven to 425 degrees F. Stir the oil, rosemary, 1 tablespoon of salt, and 1½ teaspoons of pepper in a small bowl to blend. Place the pork loin in a heavy, flame-proof roasting pan. Spread the oil mixture over the pork to coat completely. Roast, turning the pork every 15 minutes to ensure even browning, until an instant-read meat thermometer inserted into the center of the pork registers 145 degrees F, about 45 minutes total.

Transfer the pork to a cutting board and tent with foil to keep warm. Let the pork rest for 15 minutes. Meanwhile, place the roasting pan over medium heat and stir in the chicken broth, scraping the bottom of the pan to remove any browned bits. Bring the pan juices to a simmer. Season with more salt and pepper to taste.

Using a large, sharp knife, cut the pork crosswise into ¼-inch-thick slices. Arrange the pork slices on plates. Spoon the jus over. Drizzle the warm fig sauce around and serve immediately.

Roasted Pork Loin
with Fig Sauce

White Bean Dip with Pita Chips

This dip is the Italian version of hummus, and in my opinion it's smoother and tastier. This is a staple antipasto when I'm entertaining. The pita chips aren't Italian, but they work really well with this dip.

6 APPETIZER SERVINGS

  4 pita breads, split horizontally in half
  2 tablespoons plus ⅓ cup olive oil
  1 teaspoon dried oregano
1½ teaspoons salt, plus more to taste
1¼ teaspoons freshly ground black pepper, plus more to taste
  1 (15-ounce) can cannellini beans, drained and rinsed
  ¼ cup (loosely packed) fresh flat-leaf parsley leaves
  2 tablespoons fresh lemon juice (from about ½ lemon)
  1 garlic clove

Preheat the oven to 400 degrees F. Cut each pita half into 8 wedges. Arrange the pita wedges evenly over a large baking sheet. Brush the pita wedges with 2 tablespoons of the oil, then sprinkle with the oregano and 1 teaspoon each of the salt and pepper. Bake for 8 minutes, then turn the pita wedges over and bake until they are crisp and golden, about 8 minutes longer.

Meanwhile, in the bowl of a food processor, combine the beans, parsley, lemon juice, garlic, and the remaining ½ teaspoon of salt and ¼ teaspoon of pepper. Pulse on and off until the mixture is coarsely chopped. With the machine running, gradually mix in the remaining ⅓ cup of oil until the mixture is creamy. Season the purée with more salt and pepper to taste. Transfer the purée to a small bowl and serve the pita toasts warm or at room temperature alongside. (The pita wedges and bean purée can be made 1 day ahead. Store the pita wedges airtight at room temperature. Cover and refrigerate the bean purée.)

Potato Soup with Shrimp, p. 76

Paula Deen & Friends

by Paula Deen with Martha Nesbit

Southern cook Paula Deen already has one TV show, two restaurants and three cookbooks. In her latest book, she tackles her least favorite aspect of parties: "The hardest part of entertaining has never been the actual cookin' but the menu planning, which I think is a chore!" In a heavy drawl (you can almost hear it), Deen and co-author Martha Nesbit talk the reader through the menus, some more predictable and others pleasantly unexpected: "A Georgia Bulldawg Parking Lot Tailgate" and "A BIG Cocktail Buffet for Out-of-Town Wedding Guests."

Published by Simon & Schuster, 224 pages, $25.

BEST RECIPES

Potato Soup with Shrimp
76

Pecan-Coated Fish with Remoulade Sauce
78

Shrimp and Grits
80

Potato Soup with Shrimp

Potato soup is an unsung hero of the soup world; there is just nothing more belly-pleasing. As the potatoes cook, the soup thickens, leaving behind some chunks of potato. Cook the shrimp separately and add them at the last minute. They add great flavor and color, but if you don't have any shrimp on hand, the soup is still terrific without them.

¼ cup (½ stick) butter
1 small onion, diced
2 medium carrots, diced about the same size as the onion
2 tablespoons all-purpose flour
8 medium russet potatoes, peeled and cubed
4 cups milk, whole, reduced fat (2%), or low fat (1%)
2 chicken bouillon cubes, dissolved in ½ cup hot milk
1 cup half-and-half
1 teaspoon salt
¼ teaspoon pepper
1 pound medium shrimp
Crumbled bacon bits, for garnish
Grated sharp Cheddar cheese, for garnish

1. In a 4-quart saucepan, melt the butter and sauté the onion and carrots until both are slightly tender, about 5 minutes. Whisk in the flour and cook for 1 minute. Add the potatoes, milk, and dissolved bouillon cubes. Cook over medium heat for 15 minutes, until the potatoes are very soft and some of them have begun to dissolve into mush. Add the half-and-half, salt, and pepper. Let cool, then refrigerate until party time.

2. In a small saucepan, bring 2 cups lightly salted water to a boil. Add the shrimp all at once and stir well. Watch the shrimp closely; as soon as they all turn pink, turn off the heat and drain. The shrimp should be slightly undercooked. When they are cool, peel them, chop roughly into big chunks, and place them in a plastic bag. Refrigerate until party time.

3. Reheat the soup over very low heat (it will stick to the bottom of the pot if you heat it too quickly) about 45 minutes before the party. When the soup is hot, add the shrimp and stir well. Encourage your guests to sprinkle the soup with bacon bits and grated Cheddar cheese. They won't be sorry they did!

deen on her go-to cookbook

The cookbook that was really my bible when I was 18 years old and a new bride was the *Better Homes and Garden Cookbook*, in the binder with the red-and-white checked cover. I got it at one of my bridal showers and I still refer to it today!

Pecan-Coated Fish with Remoulade Sauce

A chef taught Martha how to cook fish like the restaurants do. Although this recipe calls for grouper or snapper, you could use any 1-inch-thick fish fillet. There are two steps: searing the fish on the stovetop, then completing the cooking in a preheated oven.

You can usually fit only four 6-ounce fillets in a pan, so if you're cooking for more, you'll have to use a second skillet.

SERVES 4

- 4 grouper or snapper fillets, cut about 1 inch thick, 4 to 6 ounces each
- ½ cup (1 stick) butter, melted
- 1 cup pecans, ground into crumbs in a food processor
- 1 tablespoon butter
- 1 tablespoon vegetable oil

1. Preheat the oven to 350°F.

2. Rinse the fish and pat dry. Dredge the fish in the melted butter. Spread the ground pecans on a plate and press the fish into the crumbs to coat. Turn the fillets and coat the other side.

3. In a cast-iron or other heavy, ovenproof skillet, heat the tablespoon of butter with the oil. When it begins to sizzle, sear the fish about 3 minutes per side. Place the skillet in the oven for 6 to 10 minutes, depending on the thickness of the fillets and your preference for degree of doneness. Serve immediately with Remoulade Sauce on the side.

Remoulade Sauce

This is just a snazzed up mayonnaise. It's delicious with any kind of seafood, but it's also yummy on asparagus, or on your finger!

MAKES 1½ CUPS

⅓ cup chopped fresh parsley

⅓ cup chopped green onions, white and green parts

2 tablespoons capers, with juice

1 clove garlic, minced

1 cup mayonnaise

3 tablespoons olive oil

2 tablespoons fresh lemon juice

½ teaspoon Dijon mustard

Place the parsley, green onions, capers, and garlic in a blender or food processor and combine. Add the mayonnaise, olive oil, lemon juice, and mustard. Blend well. Chill until ready to serve with seafood. This keeps in a covered container in the refrigerator for several weeks.

deen on her favorite fish

I really like to use grouper in this recipe. It's a firmer fish than snapper and it holds together a little better. I also like tilapia, which is a farm-raised fish, because it's nice and mild.

Shrimp and Grits

deen on bacon

I use applewood slab bacon for this recipe. I cut it nice and thick and it makes the most glorious shrimp and grits you've ever put in your mouth—so much better than using andouille or a smoked sausage.

Here it is, y'all! Martha's beloved shrimp and grits recipe! If you have everything chopped and measured before you start cooking, it takes only about fifteen minutes to prepare. It's perfect as a one-dish meal for a family.

SERVES 8 AS AN APPETIZER OR 4 AS A MAIN COURSE

1 cup stone-ground grits

Salt and pepper

¼ cup (½ stick) butter

2 cups shredded sharp Cheddar cheese

1 pound shrimp, peeled and deveined, left whole if small and roughly chopped if medium or large

6 slices bacon, chopped into tiny pieces

4 teaspoons fresh lemon juice

2 tablespoons chopped fresh parsley

1 cup thinly sliced green onions, white and green parts

1 large clove garlic, minced

1. In a medium saucepan, bring 4 cups water to a boil. Add the grits and salt and pepper to taste. Stir well with a whisk. Reduce the heat to the lowest possible setting and cook the grits until all the water is absorbed, about 10 to 15 minutes. Remove from the heat and stir in the butter and cheese. Keep covered until ready to serve.

2. Rinse the shrimp and pat dry. Fry the bacon in a large skillet until browned and crisp, then drain on a paper towel. Add the shrimp to the bacon grease in the skillet and sauté over medium heat just until they turn pink, about 3 minutes. Do not overcook! Immediately add the lemon juice, parsley, green onions, and garlic. Remove the skillet from the heat.

3. Pour the grits into a serving bowl. Pour the shrimp mixture over the grits. Garnish with the bacon bits.

4. If you are serving this as an appetizer, spoon ¼ cup grits onto a bread or salad plate. Top with ¼ cup of the shrimp mixture. Garnish with a sprinkling of crisp bacon bits and serve immediately.

Smoky and Fiery Skirt Steak with
Avocado-Oregano Relish, p. 84

Grilling for Life

by Bobby Flay with Stephanie Banyas and Sally Jackson

"First things first: I am not a nutritionist. I am a chef, and I am not looking to create a new diet fad," writes celebrity chef and Food Network star Bobby Flay. "What I am looking to do is to show how a healthy lifestyle can be enhanced by delicious meals from the grill." In *Grilling for Life,* Flay uses a variety of health-minded tactics: He picks lean cuts of meat like pork tenderloin and uses light coconut milk and nonfat yogurt. He also creates bold flavors—his trademark—by adding fresh herbs, spices and citrus zests to dressings, salsas and marinades. The results are all about flavor, not deprivation.

Published by Scribner, 224 pages, $22.

Find more recipes by
Bobby Flay at
foodandwine.com/flay

Smoky and Fiery Skirt Steak with Avocado-Oregano Relish

Skirt steak is a chewy cut that's full of beefy flavor. It's the perfect vehicle for the big flavors of this dressing. The smokiness comes from the chipotle chiles, which are smoked jalapeños. Make them a staple in your pantry.

SERVES 6

SMOKY AND FIERY DRESSING

- ¼ cup red wine vinegar
- 2 cloves garlic, chopped
- 2 chipotle chiles in adobo
- 1 teaspoon honey
- ¼ teaspoon kosher salt
- ¼ teaspoon freshly ground black pepper
- ½ cup canola oil
- ¼ cup finely chopped fresh cilantro leaves

Combine the vinegar, garlic, chiles, honey, salt, and pepper in a blender and blend until smooth. With the motor running, slowly drizzle in the oil and blend until emulsified. Add the cilantro and pulse 2 times just to incorporate.

AVOCADO-OREGANO RELISH

- 2 ripe Hass avocados, pitted, peeled, and coarsely chopped
- ½ medium red onion, finely chopped
- Juice of 2 limes
- 2 tablespoons canola oil
- 1 tablespoon finely chopped fresh oregano leaves
- ¼ teaspoon kosher salt
- ¼ teaspoon freshly ground black pepper

Combine all of the ingredients in a medium bowl.

GRILLED SKIRT STEAK

2 pounds skirt steak, cut crosswise into 3 equal pieces

1 tablespoon canola oil

1 teaspoon kosher salt

2 teaspoons freshly ground black pepper

1. Heat your grill to high.

2. Brush the steak with the oil and season both sides with the salt and pepper. Grill, turning once, for 6 to 8 minutes until slightly charred and cooked to medium-rare (see Temperature Guide, page 92). Transfer to a cutting board and let rest for 5 minutes.

3. Cut the meat against the grain into ½-inch-thick slices. Drizzle each serving with dressing and top with 2 tablespoons of the avocado relish. Serve the remaining relish on the side if desired.

Grilled Tuna Salad Sandwiches with Lemon-Habanero Mayonnaise

editor's note

This delicious mayonnaise would also make a perfect dipping sauce for shrimp or lobster.

SERVES 6

LEMON-HABANERO MAYONNAISE

- ¾ cup mayonnaise
- 2 tablespoons fresh lemon juice
- 2 teaspoons grated lemon zest
- ½ habanero chile, chopped
- ¼ teaspoon kosher salt
- ¼ teaspoon freshly ground black pepper
- 1 small red onion, finely chopped
- 1 large rib celery, finely chopped
- 2 tablespoons chopped fresh flat-leaf parsley leaves

Combine the mayonnaise, lemon juice, zest, and chile in a blender and blend until smooth. Season with the salt and pepper and transfer to a large bowl. Stir in the onion, celery, and parsley. Set aside while you prepare the tuna.

GRILLED TUNA SALAD SANDWICHES

- 4 tuna steaks, 8 ounces each
- 2 teaspoons olive oil
- 1 teaspoon kosher salt
- 1 teaspoon freshly ground black pepper
- 12 slices seven-grain bread
- 1 small bunch watercress

1. Heat your grill to high. Brush the tuna steaks with the oil and season both sides with the salt and pepper. Grill for 3 to 4 minutes per side until slightly charred and cooked to medium-well (see Temperature Guide, page 92).

2. Remove the tuna from the grill and transfer to a cutting board. Let rest for 5 minutes, then cut into small dice or flake with a fork. Add the tuna to the mayonnaise mixture and gently mix to combine. The tuna salad can be made up to 8 hours in advance and kept refrigerated.

3. Divide the tuna salad among 6 slices of the bread, top the salad with a few sprigs of watercress, then cover with the remaining 6 slices of bread.

Grilled Turkey Burgers with Monterey Jack, Poblano Pickle Relish, and Avocado Mayonnaise

Turkey burgers have become *the* alternative to hamburgers. Ground turkey is a great choice because of its low fat content, but that often means the burgers are dry and bland. Not these! The slightly spicy pickle relish and the cooling avocado mayonnaise infuse the burgers with flavor through and through.

SERVES 4

POBLANO PICKLE RELISH

- 2 poblano chiles, grilled (see Editor's Note, page 91), peeled, seeded, and finely chopped
- 1 large or 2 medium dill pickles, finely chopped
- 1 small red onion, finely chopped
- ¼ cup fresh lime juice
- 1 teaspoon honey
- ¼ teaspoon salt
- 2 tablespoons finely chopped fresh cilantro leaves
- ¼ teaspoon freshly ground black pepper

Combine all of the ingredients in a medium bowl. Cover and let sit at room temperature for at least 30 minutes and up to 4 hours before serving.

AVOCADO MAYONNAISE

- ½ ripe Hass avocado, peeled and chopped
- ¼ cup mayonnaise
- 1 tablespoon fresh lime juice
- 2 cloves garlic, chopped
- ½ teaspoon ground cumin
- ¼ teaspoon kosher salt
- ¼ teaspoon freshly ground black pepper

Place all of the ingredients in a food processor and process until smooth.

Grilled Turkey Burgers with Monterey Jack, Poblano Pickle Relish, and Avocado Mayonnaise (at bottom)

TURKEY BURGERS

1½ pounds ground turkey, 99% lean

 2 tablespoons canola oil

½ teaspoon kosher salt

½ teaspoon freshly ground black pepper

 4 slices Monterey Jack cheese, ½ ounce each

1. Heat your grill to high.

2. Shape the ground turkey with your hands into 4 round patties about 1½ inches thick. Brush each burger on both sides with the oil and season with the salt and pepper. Grill until slightly charred on both sides and cooked completely through (see Temperature Guide, page 92), about 4 minutes per side. Place a slice of cheese on each burger, close the lid of the grill, and cook for 1 minute longer to melt the cheese. Transfer to a cutting board and let rest for 5 minutes.

3. Top each burger with 1 tablespoon of the avocado mayonnaise and a few tablespoons of the relish. Serve the remaining avocado mayonnaise on the side if desired.

editor's note

Because these burgers are made from lean turkey meat, they can easily dry out during cooking. Take them off the heat once the internal temperature has reached 155˚ and let them rest until it rises to 160˚.

Grilled Salmon with Anchovy Vinaigrette and Grilled Pepper and Black Olive Relish

Too many people are afraid of anchovies. These little fish have gotten a bad rap, but they really are a seasoning miracle. Their pungent saltiness lends an incredible layer of flavor to this vinaigrette. With the relish, the vinaigrette provides the perfect balance for the rich, buttery salmon.

SERVES 4

GRILLED PEPPER AND BLACK OLIVE RELISH

- 2 red bell peppers, grilled (see Editor's Note, at right), peeled, seeded, and diced
- 2 yellow bell peppers, grilled (see Editor's Note, at right), peeled, seeded, and diced
- ½ cup coarsely chopped pitted Niçoise olives
- 1 tablespoon minced garlic
- ¼ cup coarsely chopped fresh flat-leaf parsley leaves
- 1 tablespoon chopped fresh thyme leaves
- ¼ cup sherry vinegar
- 2 teaspoons honey
- 1 teaspoon kosher salt
- 1 teaspoon freshly ground black pepper

Combine the peppers, olives, garlic, parsley, thyme, vinegar, and honey in a mixing bowl. Season with the salt and pepper. The relish can be made up to 1 day in advance. Bring to room temperature before serving.

ANCHOVY VINAIGRETTE

- 2 tablespoons mayonnaise
- 2 teaspoons Dijon mustard
- 1 teaspoon fresh lemon juice
- ¼ cup sherry vinegar
- ¼ teaspoon freshly ground black pepper
- 5 anchovy fillets
- 1 small shallot, coarsely chopped
- ⅓ cup olive oil

Combine the mayonnaise, mustard, lemon juice, vinegar, pepper, anchovies, and shallot in a blender and blend until smooth. With the motor running, drizzle in the oil and blend until emulsified. The vinaigrette can be made up to 8 hours in advance and kept refrigerated.

GRILLED SALMON

  4 skinless salmon fillets, 6 ounces each

  1 tablespoon olive oil

¼ teaspoon kosher salt

  1 teaspoon freshly ground black pepper

1. Heat your grill to high.

2. Brush the salmon fillets on both sides with the oil and season with the salt and pepper. Place the fillets on the grill and cook until golden brown and a crust has formed, 2 to 3 minutes. Turn the salmon over and continue grilling for 3 to 4 minutes until cooked to medium (see Temperature Guide, page 92). Remove from the grill and let rest for 5 minutes.

3. Drizzle each fillet with 2 tablespoons of the vinaigrette and top with the relish. Serve the remaining vinaigrette on the side if desired.

editor's note

Flay cooks peppers and chiles right on the grill. Heat the grill to high. Brush the peppers with olive oil and season with salt and pepper. Grill until charred on all sides, 8 to 10 minutes. Place the peppers in a bowl, cover with plastic wrap and let sit for 15 minutes. Then peel, halve, stem and seed them.

Temperature Guide for Perfect Grilling

The second most common question I get asked (after what brand of grill I recommend) is what internal temperature should poultry, pork, beef, lamb, and fish be cooked to? The following "introductory" chart contains the internal temperatures that I prefer meat and fish to reach on an instant-read thermometer. The temperatures I list are the internal temperature at which meat/fish should be taken off the grill and the temperature at which it should be served after resting. All meat/fish should rest, loosely covered with foil to keep it warm, for at least 5 minutes after grilling to redistribute the juices and finish cooking; during this time the internal temperature of the meat will increase by 5 to 10 degrees.

MEAT	REMOVE FROM HEAT	SERVING TEMPERATURE AFTER RESTING	USDA RECOMMENDS
beef steaks/lamb chops MEDIUM-RARE	130°F	135 to 140°F	150°F
ground beef/lamb MEDIUM	135°F	140 to 145°F	160°F
pork tenderloin/chops MEDIUM-WELL	145°F	150 to 155°F	170°F
chicken breast/turkey breast MEDIUM-WELL	150 to 155°F	160°F	170°F
duck breast MEDIUM-RARE	135°F	145°F	170°F
fish fillets/whole fish MEDIUM	135°F	140 to 145°F	160°F
tuna MEDIUM-RARE	120°F	125°F	160°F

BEST OF THE BEST EXCLUSIVE

Red Chile–Crusted Sea Scallops with Smoky Bacon and Lima Bean Salad

4 SERVINGS

¼ pound sliced bacon, cut crosswise into ½-inch strips

2 tablespoons pure ground ancho chile powder

1½ teaspoons ground cumin

12 large sea scallops (1 pound)

Kosher salt and freshly ground pepper

3 tablespoons extra-virgin olive oil

¼ cup red wine vinegar

3 tablespoons crème fraîche

One 10-ounce bag frozen lima beans, thawed and drained

2 tablespoons chopped cilantro

editor's note

Flay only serves this dish at his New York restaurant Mesa Grill during the spring, when he can use fresh fava beans. But he says that frozen lima beans make a great year-round substitute.

1. In a medium skillet, cook the bacon over moderately high heat until crisp, about 4 minutes. Transfer to paper towels to drain.

2. In a small bowl, mix the chile powder with the cumin. Season the scallops with salt and pepper. Dredge one side of each scallop in the chile mixture. In a large skillet, heat the olive oil until shimmering. Add the scallops, chile side down, and cook over moderately high heat until a crust forms, about 2 minutes. Turn the scallops and cook about 3 minutes longer until just cooked through. Transfer to a plate.

3. Add the vinegar to the skillet, reduce the heat to moderately low and scrape up any brown bits from the bottom of the pan. Whisk in the crème fraîche. Add the lima beans and cook until heated through, about 1 minute. Add the cilantro and bacon and season with salt and pepper. Spoon the lima beans onto plates, top with the scallops and serve.

Summer Bean Salad with
Creamy Lemon Dressing, p. 96

Eat This Book

by Tyler Florence

"*Eat This Book* is a well-stamped passport of cooking experiences that I've picked up from traveling and shooting cooking shows," writes Food Network star Tyler Florence. "And over the past two years, I've been practically everywhere." Florence's book is packed with discoveries from places like Puerto Rico, Thailand, Italy, France and Greece. What unifies these recipes is that they all feel utterly approachable, written in a familiar, friendly tone ("First get the potatoes going"), as if Florence is standing right next to you.

Published by Clarkson Potter, 288 pages, $32.50.

BEST RECIPES

Summer Bean Salad with
Creamy Lemon Dressing
96

Artichokes with Lemon,
Sausage, and Sage
97

Peach and Blueberry
Crostata
101

**BEST OF THE BEST
EXCLUSIVE**

Crisp and Buttery
Strawberry-Brie
Sandwiches
103

Find more recipes by
Tyler Florence at
foodandwine.com/florence

Summer Bean Salad with Creamy Lemon Dressing

editor's note
Toast walnuts on a baking sheet in a 375° oven for 7 to 8 minutes, until fragrant, Florence says.

I came up with this recipe last summer. I was strolling through the Union Square Greenmarket in New York City and I came across these really cool summer beans—yellow wax beans and beautiful haricots verts. I put together a simple vinaigrette with the things I had in my pantry: lemon juice, mustard, and crème fraîche. Green beans taste like a cool drink of water to me—grassy and cool. I took the bowl, sat on my fire escape in the hot July sun, and had a picnic.

SERVES 6

- 1 pound mixed summer beans, such as sugar snap peas, haricots verts or green beans, yellow wax beans, or runner beans, stems trimmed
- 1½ shallots, finely chopped
- ½ cup walnut halves and pieces, toasted (see Editor's Note, at left)
- 1 handful of fresh flat-leaf parsley, chopped
- 1 tablespoon grainy mustard
- 1 tablespoon hot water
- ½ teaspoon sugar
- Juice of 1 lemon
- ⅓ cup extra-virgin olive oil
- ¼ cup crème fraîche or sour cream
- Kosher salt and freshly ground black pepper

30 MINUTES

Bring a large pot of salted water to a boil. Add all of the beans and cook until crisp-tender, 3 to 5 minutes (they'll all be done at roughly the same time). Drain, transfer to a bowl of salted ice water to stop the cooking, and drain well. Transfer to a mixing bowl and toss in the shallots, walnuts, and parsley.

In a jar, combine the mustard, water, sugar, lemon juice, oil, crème fraîche, salt, and pepper. Put the cap on and shake vigorously to emulsify. Just before you serve the salad, pour the dressing over the beans and toss well to coat with the dressing.

Artichokes with Lemon, Sausage, and Sage

You'll find this dish served in homes in Florence throughout the Christmas holidays. It's an amalgamation of great flavors. The earthy sweet artichokes, the lemons, and sage act as supporting players to make the sausage taste amazing. This dish looks beautiful served on individual plates or passed around at the table on a big platter, family style.

SERVES 8

ARTICHOKES

 1 handful of fresh flat-leaf parsley

 4 garlic cloves

 2 bay leaves

 ¼ cup dry white wine, such as Pinot Grigio

 1 lemon, halved

Kosher salt and freshly ground black pepper

 4 whole artichokes

Extra-virgin olive oil

 4 pork sausages (6 ounces each)

 4 fresh sage leaves

 2 shallots, minced

 4 garlic cloves, minced

 ½ lemon, cut into paper-thin slices

 ½ cup chicken stock, homemade (see Rich Chicken Stock, page 100) or store-bought

 2 tablespoons unsalted butter

Chopped fresh flat-leaf parsley, for garnish

1½ HOURS

First thing to do is to steam the artichokes in a flavorful broth. Put the parsley, garlic cloves, bay leaves, wine, and lemon halves in a wide pot. Add 2 quarts of water and bring to a simmer. Season the broth with salt and pepper.

Artichokes with Lemon,
Sausage, and Sage

While that's coming to a simmer, wash the artichokes under cold water. Then, using a paring knife, trim the bottom end of each stem and shave the stem down to expose the tender, light green flesh underneath. Snap or cut off the outer petals until you reach the soft, pale green leaves in the center. Slice off about 1 inch from the top of each artichoke with a large knife.

Slide the artichokes into the simmering broth, then cover the pan and simmer over medium-low heat for about 20 minutes, until there is no resistance when a knife is inserted into the base of each artichoke. Remove the artichokes from the broth with tongs. Using a spoon, carefully scoop out the hairy choke from the center of each and discard. Try to keep the artichoke intact as best you can; it looks great for presentation.

Now go on to the rest of the dish. Put a large, deep skillet over medium heat and cover the bottom with a 2-count of oil. When the oil is smoking hot, add the sausages and cook for 7 to 10 minutes, until cooked through and browned all over. Take the sausages out of the pan and set them aside. Add a drizzle of oil to the pan. Then add the sage leaves and cook for 2 to 3 minutes to infuse the oil with their flavor. Toss in the shallots, garlic, and lemon slices and cook for 2 minutes. Add the stock to the pan, bring to a boil, lower the heat, and simmer until reduced and thickened. Swirl in the butter to emulsify, and add a drizzle of olive oil for flavor. Return the artichokes to the pan and cook over low heat for a few minutes to warm them up. Spoon the artichokes out onto plates and serve with half a sausage. Sprinkle with chopped flat-leaf parsley.

Rich Chicken Stock

MAKES 2 QUARTS

- 1 chicken (about 3½ pounds), free range if you can get it
- 1 rutabaga, cut in large chunks
- 2 carrots, cut in large chunks
- 2 celery stalks, cut in large chunks
- 2 large onions, quartered
- 1 turnip, halved
- 1 head of garlic, halved
- ¼ bunch of fresh thyme
- 2 bay leaves
- 1 teaspoon whole black peppercorns

1½ HOURS

Remove the giblets from the chicken, discarding the liver. Rinse the chicken with cool water. Put the chicken, vegetables, and giblets in a large stockpot. Pour in enough cold water to cover by 1 inch (about 3 quarts); too much will make the broth taste weak. Toss in the herbs and peppercorns and allow the stock to slowly come to a boil over medium heat. Skim off the foam, then reduce the heat and simmer gently for 1 hour, uncovered, until the chicken is cooked through. As the stock cooks, skim any impurities that rise to the surface; add more water if necessary to keep the chicken covered while simmering.

Carefully remove the chicken to a cutting board. When it is cool enough to handle, discard the skin and bones; shred the meat by hand into a storage container and reserve for soups or salads.

In the meantime, set a large, fine-mesh sieve or a large strainer lined with cheesecloth over another pot. Pour the stock into the sieve to strain out the solids; discard. Use the stock immediately or, if you plan on storing it, place the pot in a sink of ice water and stir to cool down the stock. Transfer to a container, cover, and refrigerate for up to 1 week, or freeze.

Peach and Blueberry Crostata

SERVES 6 TO 8

PASTRY DOUGH

- 2 cups all-purpose flour, plus more for rolling
- 3 tablespoons sugar
- ¼ teaspoon salt

Zest of 1 lemon, finely grated

- ¾ cup (1½ sticks) cold, unsalted butter, cut into small chunks
- 1 large egg yolk
- 2 tablespoons ice water, plus more if needed

FILLING

- 4 large ripe peaches
- 1 pint fresh blueberries

Juice of ½ lemon

- 2 tablespoons sugar
- 2 teaspoons all-purpose flour

- 1 large egg, beaten with a drizzle of cold water
- 2 tablespoons sugar

Vanilla ice cream, for serving

1½ HOURS

Combine the flour, sugar, salt, and lemon zest in a large mixing bowl. Add the butter and mix with a pastry blender or your fingers until the mixture resembles coarse crumbs. Add the egg yolk and the ice water and work that in with your hands. (Or do the whole thing in the food processor, pulsing a couple of times to combine the dry ingredients, pulsing in the butter, and then the egg and water.) You want there to be just enough moisture to bind the dough so that it holds together without being too wet or sticky, so check the consistency: squeeze a small amount of the dough together between your thumb and forefingers. If it's still crumbly, add a little more ice water, 1 teaspoon at a time.

florence on his inspirations

I carry around a little pad with me all the time, like a flavor journal, and if I taste something really great or think about a good flavor combination, I'll write it down. Eventually, that'll turn into a recipe.

Peach and Blueberry Crostata

When you get it to the right consistency, shape the dough into a disk and wrap it in plastic. Put it in the refrigerator and chill for at least 30 minutes.

When the dough has chilled, preheat the oven to 450°F. Put a pizza stone in the oven to heat, if you have one.

Cut the peaches in half, discard the pits, slice in a large bowl. Add the blueberries, lemon juice, sugar, and flour and toss to coat; set aside.

Sprinkle the counter and a rolling pin lightly with flour. Roll the dough out to a 14-inch round, about ¼ inch thick. It doesn't have to be a perfect circle; free form is good. Transfer the dough to a lightly floured pizza paddle. (If you don't have a pizza stone and paddle, transfer to the back of a jelly-roll pan; you'll put that right in the oven.) Spoon the filling mixture over the center of the dough round, leaving a 2-inch border all around. Brush the border with the egg wash. Bring the edge of crust over onto the filling, leaving the fruit exposed in the center. Gently fold and pinch the dough to seal any cracks. Brush the crust with the remaining egg wash and sprinkle with the sugar. Transfer to the pizza stone (or put the pan in the oven) and bake for 30 minutes, or until the crust is golden brown and the fruit is bubbly and tender. Slide a knife under the tart to loosen it from the stone or pan. Then cut into wedges and serve warm or at room temperature with vanilla ice cream.

BEST OF THE BEST EXCLUSIVE

Crisp and Buttery Strawberry-Brie Sandwiches

4 SERVINGS

Eight 1-inch-thick slices of brioche

3 tablespoons unsalted butter, softened

2 tablespoons granulated sugar

¼ cup strawberry jam

6 ounces strawberries, hulled and thinly sliced (1 cup)

6 ounces Brie cheese, cut into ¼-inch slices, at room temperature

Confectioners' sugar, for serving

1. Arrange the brioche slices on a work surface. Butter one side of each slice, using 2 tablespoons of the butter. Sprinkle the granulated sugar over the buttered brioche. Turn 4 of the slices buttered side down; spread those slices with the strawberry jam. Top the jam with the sliced strawberries and the Brie. Cover the Brie sandwiches with the remaining brioche, buttered side up.

2. In a large nonstick skillet, melt the remaining 1 tablespoon of butter over moderate heat. Add the sandwiches and cook, turning once and pressing them with the back of a spatula, until the brioche is golden and the Brie is melted, about 6 minutes. Transfer the sandwiches to plates, dust with confectioners' sugar and serve.

editor's note
This buttery sweet riff on a grilled cheese sandwich would make a decadent brunch accompanied by a glass of Champagne. This recipe will appear in the forthcoming book, *Tyler's Ultimate at Home.*

Goin receives a delivery of local produce for her Los Angeles restaurant Lucques.

Sunday Suppers at Lucques

by Suzanne Goin with Teri Gelber

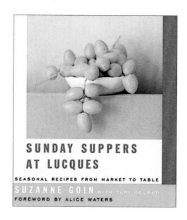

Ever since opening her Los Angeles restaurant Lucques eight years ago, chef Suzanne Goin has served casual, fixed-price Sunday suppers that remind her of the meals she ate with her family when she was growing up. This excellent book is a compilation of her favorites. The recipes are tempting, innovative and absolutely doable. Despite the homey title, this is an indispensable cookbook for anyone who likes to entertain—on Sundays or any night of the week.

Published by Alfred A. Knopf, 416 pages, $35.

BEST RECIPES

Wild Salmon Salad with Beets, Potato, Egg, and Mustard Vinaigrette
106

Green Goddess Salad with Romaine, Cucumbers, and Avocado
109

Lamb Skewers with Lima Bean Purée and French Feta Salsa Verde
111

Devil's Chicken Thighs with Braised Leeks and Dijon Mustard
114

BEST OF THE BEST EXCLUSIVE

Red Cabbage Salad with Apples, Bacon and Pecans
117

Find more recipes by Suzanne Goin at **foodandwine.com/goin**

Wild Salmon Salad with Beets, Potato, Egg, and Mustard Vinaigrette

goin on the best greens

You don't have to special-order dandelion greens to make this salad. If you go to the market and find amazing baby mustard greens, or arugula, or watercress, then go ahead and use that.

Inspired by main-course salads found in the bistros of France, this dish comprises some of my favorite ingredients—beets, mustard, dandelion, and soft-boiled egg. The salmon is covered in minced herbs, seasoned with *fleur de sel,* and then slow-roasted in a humid oven until it's moist and custardlike at the center.

3 bunches beets, preferably mixed colors

6 tablespoons extra-virgin olive oil

1 pound very small potatoes

1 teaspoon thyme leaves

2 pounds wild salmon (1 piece), skin on, bones removed

1 lemon

½ cup finely diced shallots

2 tablespoons minced dill

2 teaspoons minced tarragon

¼ cup minced flat-leaf parsley

½ teaspoon *fleur de sel*

3 extra-large eggs

Dijon Mustard Vinaigrette (recipe follows)

4 ounces young dandelion greens, cleaned and dried

Kosher salt and freshly ground black pepper

Preheat the oven to 400°F.

Cut the greens from the beets, leaving ½ inch of stem still attached. (Save the leaves for sautéing later; they are delicious!) Clean the beets well, and toss them with 2 tablespoons olive oil and 1 teaspoon salt.

Place the beets in a roasting pan with a splash of water. Cover tightly with foil, and roast about 40 minutes, until tender when pierced. (The roasting time will depend on the size and type of beet.) When the beets are done, carefully remove the foil. Let cool, and peel the beets by slipping off the skins with your fingers. Cut the beets into ½-inch wedges.

While the beets are in the oven, toss the potatoes with 1 tablespoon olive oil, the thyme, and 1 teaspoon salt. Place in a roasting pan, cover with foil, and cook in the oven about 30 minutes, until tender when pierced. When the potatoes have cooled, cut them in half.

Remove the salmon from the refrigerator 30 minutes before cooking, to bring it to room temperature.

Turn the oven down to 250°F and place a shallow pan of water on the bottom rack.

Finely grate the zest of the lemon until you have 1 teaspoon. Combine the lemon zest, shallots, dill, tarragon, and parsley in a small bowl, and stir in 2 tablespoons olive oil.

Place the salmon, skin side down, on a baking sheet, and season with 2 teaspoons kosher salt and some freshly ground black pepper. Smear about a third of the herb mixture on the fish, and turn it over. Slather the skin side of the fish with the remaining herb mixture, and season with the *fleur de sel* and a little more black pepper.

Place the salmon on a wire rack set on a baking sheet, or in a roasting pan. Bake the salmon about 25 minutes, until medium-rare to medium. The center will still be slightly translucent. To check if the salmon is done, peek between the flakes. If it doesn't separate into flakes, it's not ready yet.

Meanwhile, bring a small pot of water to a boil, and carefully lower the eggs into the pot. Turn the heat down to low, and gently simmer exactly 9 minutes. Immediately transfer the eggs to a bowl of ice water to stop the cooking. When they're completely cooled, peel the eggs, and cut them into halves. Season with salt and pepper.

Season the beets with a healthy pinch of salt, a pinch of pepper, the remaining tablespoon olive oil, and a squeeze of lemon juice. Season the potatoes with ½ teaspoon salt and 2 tablespoons Dijon Mustard Vinaigrette. Taste both for seasoning.

Scatter the dandelion greens on a large platter, and drizzle ¼ cup mustard vinaigrette over them. Nestle the potatoes and beets in and around the greens. Using your hands, pull the salmon into 2-inch chunks, tucking them throughout the salad. Spoon another ¼ cup vinaigrette over the salad, and tuck the eggs in and around the other ingredients. Season the salad with a healthy squeeze of lemon juice, and pass the rest of the vinaigrette at the table.

NOTE Although there are a lot of components to this dish, the herb marinade, beets, potatoes, eggs, and mustard vinaigrette can be prepared ahead of time and dressed at the last minute. Even the salmon can be baked an hour or two before serving, since it's served at room temperature.

Dijon Mustard Vinaigrette

1 extra-large egg yolk

1 tablespoon Dijon mustard

1½ tablespoons red wine vinegar

1 tablespoon lemon juice

¾ cup extra-virgin olive oil

Kosher salt and freshly ground black pepper

Whisk the egg yolk in a small bowl with the mustard, red wine vinegar, lemon juice, ½ teaspoon salt, and a pinch of pepper. Slowly whisk in the olive oil. Thin the vinaigrette with 1 teaspoon water or more if needed. Taste for balance and seasoning.

Green Goddess Salad
with Romaine, Cucumbers,
and Avocado

I love dishes with catchy retro names. The Green Goddess salad was invented in the 1920s by the chef of the Palace Hotel in San Francisco, who made it in honor of British actor George Arliss. The actor was a guest at the hotel while starring in a local production of William Archer's *The Green Goddess*.

The basic components of this classic California dressing are anchovies, mayonnaise, garlic, tarragon, parsley, and chives. I add watercress to the puréed herbs, which turns the dressing a deep emerald green and adds a clean, peppery flavor. Thick and rich, the dressing coats the romaine leaves the same way a Caesar salad dressing does. Once you have this dressing in your repertoire, you'll find yourself using it for all sorts of things. Try a dollop over grilled fish, or spread it on bread instead of mayonnaise when making a sandwich.

- 2 large heads romaine lettuce
- 1 extra-large egg yolk
- 1 cup grapeseed oil
- 1¼ cups flat-leaf parsley leaves
- 1 cup packed watercress, cleaned, tough stems removed
- 2 tablespoons tarragon leaves
- 3 tablespoons minced chives, plus 2 tablespoons ½-inch-snipped chives
- 1 clove garlic, chopped
- 2 salt-packed anchovies, rinsed, bones removed
- Juice of 1 lemon
- 1 tablespoon plus 1 teaspoon champagne vinegar
- 2 large ripe avocados, preferably Reed, Hass, or Bacon
- 3 Persian cucumbers or 1 hothouse cucumber
- Kosher salt and freshly ground black pepper

Remove the tough outer leaves of the romaine. Trim the root and core and separate the leaves. Tear the larger leaves in half. Clean by submerging in cold water. Spin dry, and chill in the refrigerator.

goin on grapeseed oil

I really like to use grapeseed oil for this recipe because it's flavorless. You can use any kind of flavorless oil, like vegetable oil. I'm a huge olive oil fan, but if you made this recipe with olive oil, it would overwhelm all the other flavors.

Place the egg yolk in a stainless-steel bowl. Slowly pour ¼ cup of the oil in the bowl, drop by drop, whisking all the time. Continue in this manner as the mixture thickens. Once the mayonnaise has emulsified, whisk in another ¼ cup oil in a slow, steady stream.

Purée 1 cup parsley leaves, the watercress, tarragon, and minced chives in a blender with the garlic, anchovies, lemon juice, and remaining ½ cup oil.

Whisk the herb purée, vinegar, 2 teaspoons salt, and ½ teaspoon pepper into the mayonnaise. If the dressing seems too thick, thin it with a little water. Taste for balance and seasoning.

Cut each avocado in half lengthwise, remove the pit, and peel. Slice into long wedges. Taste the cucumbers and peel and seed them if necessary. Cut the cucumbers in half lengthwise, and cut them on the diagonal into ¼-inch-thick slices. Season the avocado and cucumber generously with salt and pepper.

Place the romaine in a large salad bowl, and toss with 1 cup dressing, ¼ teaspoon salt, and some more black pepper. Gently toss in the avocado and cucumber. Arrange on a large chilled platter, and scatter the remaining ¼ cup parsley leaves and the snipped chives over the top.

Lamb Skewers with Lima Bean Purée and French Feta Salsa Verde

  6 branches rosemary, about 7 to 8 inches long

2½ pounds lamb sirloin

  3 cloves garlic, smashed

  1 tablespoon thyme leaves

  2 teaspoons cracked black pepper

  ¼ pound French feta cheese, crumbled

  1 recipe Salsa Verde (recipe follows)

  ½ lemon, for juicing

  2 tablespoons extra-virgin olive oil

Lima Bean Purée (recipe follows)

  1 bunch dandelion or arugula, cleaned

Kosher salt and freshly ground black pepper

Remove all the rosemary leaves from the branches except 2 inches' worth at the top of each. Cut the leafless end of the branch at an angle with a sharp knife to make a point (this will make it easier to skewer the lamb). Coarsely chop the rosemary leaves you removed from the branches.

Cut the lamb into 1-to-1½-inch-thick 2-ounce pieces.

Season the lamb with 2 tablespoons chopped rosemary leaves, the smashed garlic, thyme, and cracked black pepper. Cover, and refrigerate at least 4 hours, preferably overnight.

Light the grill 30 to 40 minutes before cooking, and take the lamb out of the refrigerator so it comes to room temperature.

Skewer three pieces of lamb onto each rosemary branch. The pieces on each skewer should be of similar thickness and not skewered too tightly or they will not cook evenly.

Stir the feta into the salsa verde. Taste for seasoning. It does not usually need salt but might need lemon and a pinch of pepper. Set aside.

When the coals are broken down, red, and glowing, brush the lamb skewers with olive oil, and season generously with salt. Place the lamb on the grill, and

The rosemary skewers
are pretty and they
flavor the lamb as it's
cooking. If you can't
find rosemary branches,
then a regular wooden
skewer will work fine.

cook 3 minutes on each side, rotating the skewers a few times to get nice color, until they're medium-rare.

Spoon the warm Lima Bean Purée onto a large warm platter. Scatter the dandelion greens over it, and arrange the skewers on top. Spoon some of the French Feta Salsa Verde over the lamb, and serve the rest on the side.

Lima Bean Purée

½ cup extra-virgin olive oil

1 small sprig rosemary

1 dried chile de árbol, crumbled

2 teaspoons minced garlic

2 cups cooked fresh lima beans, well-drained

½ lemon, for juicing

Kosher salt and freshly ground black pepper

Heat a medium saucepan over medium heat for 1 minute. Pour in the olive oil and turn the heat down to low. Add the rosemary sprig and the crumbled chile. When the rosemary begins to sizzle, add the garlic. Cook a minute or so, then add the lima beans and ½ teaspoon salt. Stew gently 5 to 7 minutes, until the beans are soft but not mushy. Strain the beans, reserving the oil. Discard the rosemary sprig and chile.

Place the beans in a food processor and purée. With the motor running, slowly pour in some of the reserved oil until the mixture has a smooth consistency. You may not need all the oil. Season with salt, pepper, and a squeeze of lemon to taste.

Salsa Verde

1 teaspoon marjoram or oregano leaves

¼ cup coarsely chopped mint

1 cup coarsely chopped flat-leaf parsley

¾ cup extra-virgin olive oil

1 small clove garlic

1 salt-packed anchovy, rinsed, bones removed

1 tablespoon salt-packed capers, rinsed and drained

½ lemon, for juicing

Freshly ground black pepper

Using a mortar and pestle, pound the herbs to a paste. (You may have to do this in batches.) Work in some of the olive oil, and transfer the mixture to a bowl. Pound the garlic and anchovy, and add them to the herbs.

Gently pound the capers until they're partially crushed, and add them to the herbs. Stir in the remaining oil, a pinch of black pepper, and a squeeze of lemon juice. Taste for balance and seasoning.

**goin on
anchovies**

I like salt-packed anchovies because I think they taste cleaner and better than the variety that's kept in oil. I think that oil-packed anchovies get kind of fishy tasting in an unpleasant way.

Devil's Chicken Thighs with Braised Leeks and Dijon Mustard

editor's note

Goin says that elements of this dish can be made a day ahead. The leeks can be braised the day before and the chicken tastes best when marinated overnight.

12 chicken thighs, trimmed of excess skin and fat

 1 cup thinly sliced onion

 3 tablespoons plus 1 teaspoon thyme leaves

 2 chiles de árbol, thinly sliced on the diagonal

 2 fresh bay leaves, thinly sliced, or 2 dried leaves, crumbled

¾ cup dry vermouth

 2 cups fresh breadcrumbs

 5 tablespoons unsalted butter

 2 tablespoons chopped flat-leaf parsley

½ cup finely diced shallots

½ cup Dijon mustard

 1 extra-large egg

 2 teaspoons chopped tarragon

 2 tablespoons extra-virgin olive oil

Braised Leeks (recipe follows)

¾ cup chicken stock

Kosher salt and freshly ground black pepper

Place the chicken thighs in a large bowl with the sliced onion, 2 tablespoons thyme, chiles, bay leaves, and ¼ cup vermouth. Using your hands, toss to coat the chicken well. Cover, and refrigerate at least 4 hours, preferably overnight.

Place the breadcrumbs in a medium bowl. Heat a large sauté pan over medium heat for 1 minute. Add 3 tablespoons butter, and cook until it's brown and smells nutty. Use a rubber spatula to scrape the brown butter over the breadcrumbs. Wait 1 minute, and then toss well with the parsley and 1 tablespoon thyme.

Preheat the oven to 375°F.

Return the sauté pan to medium heat for 1 minute. Swirl in the remaining 2 tablespoons butter, and when it foams, add the shallots and remaining 1 teaspoon thyme. Sauté about 2 minutes, until the shallots are translucent. Add the remaining ½ cup vermouth and reduce by half. Transfer to a bowl and let cool a few minutes. Whisk in the mustard, egg, chopped tarragon, and a pinch of black pepper.

Remove the chicken from the refrigerator 30 minutes before cooking, to bring it to room temperature. Discard the seasonings, and pat the chicken dry with paper towels. After 15 minutes, season the thighs well on both sides with salt and pepper.

Return the same sauté pan to high heat for about 2 minutes. Swirl in the olive oil, and wait 1 minute. Place the chicken thighs in the pan, skin side down, and cook 8 to 10 minutes, until the skin is a deep golden brown. Turn the thighs over, and cook a minute or two on the other side. Place the chicken on the braised leeks. Turn off the heat and discard the fat. Add the chicken stock to the pan, and scrape with a wooden spoon to release the crispy bits stuck to the bottom. Pour the chicken stock over the braised leeks.

Toss the chicken thighs in the bowl with the mustard mixture, slathering them completely, and then rearrange them over the braised leeks. Spoon any remaining mustard mixture over the chicken thighs. Top each thigh with breadcrumbs, patting with your hands to make sure they get nicely coated. (You want lots of mustard mixture and lots of breadcrumbs.) Bake about 40 minutes, until the chicken is just cooked through. To check for doneness, pierce the meat near the bone with a paring knife; when ready, the juices from the chicken will run clear.

Turn the oven up to 475°F and cook the chicken thighs another 10 minutes, until the breadcrumbs are golden brown.

Serve in the baking dish, or transfer to a large warm platter.

editor's note

Goin explains that you will most likely need to sauté the leeks in batches or in a couple of pans, adding oil as needed.

Braised Leeks

6 large leeks

About ¾ cup extra-virgin olive oil

1 cup sliced shallots

1 tablespoon thyme leaves

½ cup dry white wine

1½ to 2 cups chicken or vegetable stock or water

Kosher salt and freshly ground black pepper

Preheat the oven to 400°F.

Remove any bruised outer layers from the leeks. Trim off to the roots, leaving the root end intact. Trim the tops of the leeks on the diagonal, leaving 2 inches of the green part attached. Cut the leeks in half lengthwise, and submerge in a large bowl of cold water to clean them. Shake the leeks well to dislodge the dirt stuck inside. Let them sit a few minutes to allow any grit inside the layers to fall to the bottom of the bowl. Repeat the process until the water is clean. Place the leeks, cut side down, on a towel and pat dry completely.

Turn the leeks over so their cut sides are facing up, and season with 2 teaspoons salt and a few grindings of black pepper.

Heat a large sauté pan over medium-high heat for 2 minutes. Pour in ¼ cup olive oil, and wait 1 minute. Place the leeks in the pan, cut side down, being careful not to crowd them. Sear them 4 to 5 minutes, until golden brown. Season the backs of the leeks with salt and pepper, and turn them over to cook another 3 to 4 minutes. Transfer to a large gratin dish, cut sides facing up.

Pour ¼ cup olive oil into the pan and heat over medium heat. Add the shallots, thyme, ¼ teaspoon salt, and a pinch of pepper. Cook about 5 minutes, until the shallots are just beginning to color. Add the white wine and reduce by half. Add 1½ cups stock, and bring to a boil over high heat. Pour the liquid over the leeks. The stock should not quite cover them; add more stock if necessary. Braise in the oven 30 minutes, until the leeks are tender when pierced.

BEST OF THE BEST EXCLUSIVE

Red Cabbage Salad with Apples, Bacon and Pecans

6 SERVINGS

One ½-inch-thick slice of bakery white bread, crusts removed,
   bread torn into pieces

1½ teaspoons extra-virgin olive oil

½ cup pecans

¼ pound bacon in one piece, sliced lengthwise ½ inch thick and
   crosswise into ¼-inch lardons

1½ pounds red cabbage, cored and finely shredded

 1 red onion, halved lengthwise and thinly sliced crosswise

1½ teaspoons fresh thyme

 2 tablespoons red wine vinegar

Kosher salt and freshly ground pepper

1½ tablespoons whole-grain mustard

 1 Fuji apple—halved, cored and cut into 2-by-¼-inch matchsticks

editor's note

Goin likes to serve
this warm wintry
cabbage salad as
an accompaniment
to pork confit,
pork chops or duck.

1. Preheat the oven to 375°. In a food processor, pulse the bread to coarse
crumbs. Transfer the crumbs to a pie plate and toss with the olive oil. Bake
for 5 minutes, stirring once, until golden and crisp. Spread the pecans in
another pie plate, and toast for 8 minutes, stirring once, until fragrant and
golden. Transfer the pecans to a plate to cool, then coarsely chop them.

2. In a large, deep skillet, cook the bacon over moderately high heat, stirring
occasionally, until lightly browned but still chewy, about 5 minutes. Stir in the
red cabbage, onion and thyme. Add the vinegar and cook until the cabbage is
wilted but still crunchy, about 5 minutes. Season with salt and pepper.

3. In a large bowl, toss the cabbage with the mustard. Add the apple and toss
gently. Sprinkle the salad with the toasted pecans and bread crumbs and serve.

Maryland Blue crabs make
a perfect dumpling.

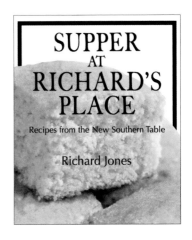

Supper at Richard's Place

by Richard Jones

"Customers have been asking me to write a cookbook for years, and now I've finally gotten around to putting my recipes down on paper," says Georgia-raised chef Richard Jones. In his first book, Jones explains how to make the soulful, homey dishes he's been preparing for 12 years at his Queens, New York, restaurant, Richard's Place. The nearly 150 recipes include modern dishes like Crabmeat Dumplings and lightened ones like Watermelon Salsa, but Jones's terrific comfort-food—including multiple variations on macaroni and cheese—is the heart of this book.

Published by Pelican, 160 pages, $21.

BEST RECIPES

Seafood Gumbo
120

Crabmeat Dumplings
121

Barbecue Rib Eye Steak
122

Oatmeal Pancakes
Stuffed with Chicken
Strips, Topped
with Pecan Syrup
123

**BEST OF THE BEST
EXCLUSIVE**

Creamy Gorgonzola
Pasta Primavera
125

Seafood Gumbo

editor's note

Many traditional recipes for gumbo call for filé powder—a spice made from the dried ground leaves of the sassafras tree—to thicken the dish. Jones notes that the powder can be hard to find, so he likes to thicken this one-pot dish with flour and okra.

My mother-in-law was born in New Orleans and reared in Mobile, Alabama. Her elder relatives orally passed on many of their cultural traditions, from generation to generation. She frequently heard stories about how the African-Creole cooks transformed the kitchens in Southern Louisiana, enriching dishes with a variety of new flavors and cooking techniques. Gumbo was one of the dishes that her relatives believed originated in the African-Creole kitchen.

MAKES 12 SERVINGS

- 8 oz. unsalted butter
- 1 cup all-purpose flour
- 2 medium onions, chopped
- 1 medium green pepper, chopped
- One 14½-oz. can stewed tomatoes
- ½ lb. fresh okra, cut in small disks
- 1½ qt. chicken stock
- 8 oz. clam juice
- 2 tsp. chopped fresh garlic
- 2 lb. medium-size shrimp, peeled and deveined
- 1 lb. lump crabmeat (or crab claw meat), picked over to remove cartilage
- Salt and black pepper to taste
- 1 bunch chopped scallions
- 2 tbsp. chopped fresh parsley

Over medium heat, melt butter in a 4- or 5-quart pot. Add flour, stirring constantly until roux is dark brown. Add onions, green pepper, stewed tomatoes, and okra. Continue to cook for approximately five minutes. Add chicken stock and clam juice. Add garlic, shrimp, and crabmeat. Cover pot and reduce heat to a simmer. Continue to cook for approximately 20 minutes. Add salt and pepper to taste. Garnish with scallions and chopped parsley.

Crabmeat Dumplings

MAKES 8 SERVINGS

2½ cups all-purpose flour

2 tsp. baking powder

¼ tsp. salt

1 tsp. seafood seasoning

¼ tsp. black pepper

¼ lb. unsalted butter

½ cup minced onions

½ cup milk

1 tbsp. Dijon mustard

2 tbsp. mayonnaise

4 large eggs

2 cups crabmeat, all shells and cartilage removed

Combine all dry ingredients in a medium bowl. Set aside. Using low heat, melt butter in a medium saucepan. Add minced onions. Cook onions for approximately 2 minutes until onions are tender. Do not brown onions. Remove saucepan from heat. Add milk, mustard, and mayonnaise to saucepan (still removed from heat). Mix ingredients well. Add eggs and beat for about two minutes. Add mixture to dry ingredients. Mix well. Fold in crabmeat. Mixture should resemble consistency of mashed potatoes. To cook the dumplings, using a teaspoon, drop batter into a rack in a steamer. Steam dumplings until cooked, approximately 8 to 10 minutes.

jones on crabmeat

If you're on a budget, I recommend using a mix of crab claw meat and lump crabmeat. The claw meat is about $10 less per pound than lump crabmeat and you won't know the difference.

Barbecue Rib Eye Steak

MAKES 2 SERVINGS

- 1 tsp. minced garlic
- 2 sprigs of rosemary
- 1 cup olive oil
- 2 12-oz. rib eye steaks
- 2 oz. sweet butter
- 1 tbsp. grated Spanish onion
- 1 tsp. minced fresh garlic
- ¼ cup sugar
- 8 oz. Worcestershire sauce
- 1¼ cup ketchup
- 1 tsp. Dijon mustard
- 1 tsp. yellow mustard
- ½ tsp. jerk seasoning
- 1 tbsp. white vinegar

Salt and pepper to taste

Combine garlic, rosemary, and olive oil in a bowl. Place steaks in mixture and marinate for 1 hour before cooking. On low heat, melt butter in a small saucepan. Add grated onions, minced garlic, and sugar. Using a wooden spoon, stir mixture for approximately 3 minutes. Add remaining ingredients. Allow sauce to simmer 8 minutes, stirring occasionally.

Heat cast-iron skillet with grill marks until skillet is very hot. Remove steak from marinade and pat semi dry. Place steaks into hot skillet and cook to desired temperature. Baste steak with barbecue sauce to taste.

Oatmeal Pancakes Stuffed with Chicken Strips, Topped with Pecan Syrup

MAKES 4 SERVINGS

FOR THE CHICKEN STRIPS

- 4 chicken cutlets
- Salt and pepper to taste
- 1 lb. all-purpose flour
- 2 cups canola oil

Cut each chicken cutlet into 3 strips and season with salt and pepper. Dredge the chicken in flour and shake off excess.

Pour oil into heavy iron skillet and heat over medium-high heat. Place chicken strips into hot oil. Fry chicken until bottom is golden brown. Using tongs, turn the chicken and brown on other side. Lower the heat if necessary to avoid burning. Continue to cook the chicken for approximately 5 to 7 minutes, turning once or twice until fully cooked. Remove chicken from pan and drain well on paper towels.

FOR THE OATMEAL PANCAKES

- 1½ cups self-rising flour
- 1 tsp. baking powder
- 1 cup old-fashioned oats
- 1 tsp. baking soda
- 4 tbsp. sugar
- 1 tsp. salt
- 3 cups buttermilk
- 2 large eggs
- 1 tsp. vanilla extract
- 4 oz. melted sweet butter
- 3 oz. canola oil to grease griddle

In a medium bowl, mix all dry ingredients together. Set aside. In a medium bowl, combine buttermilk, eggs, and vanilla extract. Using a wire whisk, whip ingredients together for approximately 1 minute. Add dry ingredients to

If you don't have
time to make the
chicken strips, you can
use pan-fried chicken
sausages instead.

buttermilk mixture. Add melted butter and continue to mix until batter is fairly smooth. Allow pancake mixture to rest for 10 minutes before cooking.

For each pancake, pour approximately ¼ cup batter onto lightly-greased griddle. Turn pancake when edges look brown and bubbles appear on top. Turn each pancake one time. Remove pancakes from griddle.

To stuff pancakes, place each pancake on a plate. Place one chicken strip on edge of each pancake and roll each pancake until thoroughly wrapped around chicken strip. Place crease down on plate. Use pecan syrup recipe for added treat.

FOR THE PECAN SYRUP

- 8 oz. melted sweet butter
- 1 cup pecans
- 16 oz. maple syrup

Place melted butter in a medium saucepan over medium heat. Add pecans and maple syrup. Stir mixture. Simmer for approximately 5 minutes or until syrup is hot. Spoon over stuffed pancakes.

BEST OF THE BEST EXCLUSIVE

Creamy Gorgonzola Pasta Primavera

editor's note

This recipe is very flexible—peas, asparagus and zucchini work just as well as the broccoli, peppers and carrots.

6 SERVINGS

½ pound broccoli, cut into 1-inch florets

1 pound penne

2 tablespoons unsalted butter

2 tablespoons extra-virgin olive oil

1 red onion, halved and thinly sliced

1 medium carrot, finely julienned

½ green bell pepper, sliced ¼ inch thick

½ red bell pepper, sliced ¼ inch thick

¼ pound cremini mushrooms, thinly sliced

1 large garlic clove, minced

1 cup chicken stock or low-sodium broth

Kosher salt and freshly ground pepper

¼ cup freshly grated Parmesan cheese

3 ounces Gorgonzola cheese, cut into ½-inch pieces (⅓ cup)

1. Bring a large pot of salted water to a boil. Add the broccoli and cook until crisp tender, about 2 minutes. Using a slotted spoon, transfer the broccoli to a bowl. In the same pot, cook the penne until al dente. Drain, reserving ¼ cup of the pasta cooking water.

2. Meanwhile, in a very large, deep skillet, melt the butter in the olive oil. Add the onion, carrot, green and red bell peppers and the mushrooms and cook over moderate heat until tender, about 5 minutes. Add the broccoli and the garlic and cook for 1 minute. Add the penne, the reserved pasta cooking water and the chicken stock and season with salt and pepper. Cook over moderate heat, stirring frequently, until the sauce coats the pasta, about 2 minutes. Remove from the heat and add the Parmesan and all but 1 tablespoon of the Gorgonzola. Toss until the cheeses are melted and the sauce is creamy. Transfer the pasta to a large serving bowl, sprinkle with the remaining Gorgonzola and serve.

Pan-Fried Halloumi Salad with Olive
and Lemon Dressing, p. 128

Small Bites

by Jennifer Joyce

In her third cookbook, *Small Bites,* ex-caterer Jennifer Joyce picks up on the restaurant trend for small plates and shows how to take advantage of it when entertaining at home. Although creating lots of smaller dishes may seem time-consuming, Joyce keeps it simple with plenty of shortcuts. Each recipe fits on a single page, includes make-ahead tips and is accompanied by a photograph. Themed menus—for an Indian feast, a Middle Eastern meal and a Latin fiesta, for instance—show how to turn these little dishes into fun parties.

Published by DK Publishing, 224 pages, $20.

Pan-Fried Halloumi Salad
with Olive and Lemon Dressing

Halloumi is a hard Cypriot cheese made from goat and sheep milk. Golden and soft when pan-fried, its salty flavor is balanced by a lemon olive dressing. If you can't find halloumi in your supermarket, you can replace it with mozzarella or order it online.

MAKES 8 SMALL SALADS OR 16 LARGE APPETIZERS

DRESSING

  3 tbsp extra-virgin olive oil

10 mild black olives, pitted and finely chopped

Medium bunch flat-leaf parsley, finely chopped

  1 tsp capers, rinsed and chopped

½ preserved lemon, rind only, rinsed and finely chopped

  2 tsp red wine vinegar

  1 small red onion, finely diced

  2 blood or navel oranges

  1 lb halloumi, drained

  1 cup flour

Salt and pepper, to taste

  4 tbsp olive oil

Small bunch flat-leaf parsley, chopped

PREPARATION TIME: 30 MINUTES

1. Put all the dressing ingredients in a small bowl, mix together, and set aside. Cut off the peel from the oranges, removing the white pith at the same time. Separate the segments by cutting between the inner membranes with a small serrated knife.

2. Cut the halloumi (or mozzarella) into 16 pieces approximately ½ inch thick and 1¼ inch by 1¼ inch square. Dust them with the flour and season with salt and pepper. Heat the olive oil over medium-high heat in a frying pan until very hot. Add the cheese to the pan in stages, and fry until colored and crispy on both sides. Add more oil if the pan becomes too dry.

3. Arrange small stacks of cheese and orange, then drizzle on the dressing and sprinkle with parsley. Alternatively, scatter the cheese and orange on a serving dish with the dressing and parsley.

PREPARE AHEAD The dressing can be made the day before. The oranges can be segmented and refrigerated on the morning you plan to serve it. The cheese can be pan-fried 1 hour before serving, then reheated or served at room temperature.

joyce on halloumi

Halloumi is a really useful cheese because it's so resilient. You can actually pan-fry it an hour in advance and let it sit out on paper towels because it tastes great at room temperature. If you want to reheat it, just blast it really quickly in a 400° oven for a few minutes.

Arabian Salad
with Dill and Crispy Pita

joyce on deseeding pomegranates

joyce on deseeding pomegranates

The best way to remove pomegranate seeds is to start by cutting the fruit in half. Then get a big mixing bowl and a large, heavy wooden spoon, hold the pomegranate cut-side down over the bowl and bash the sides of the fruit with the spoon—the seeds just come flying out.

This lively and colorful salad is a superb addition to any Middle Eastern or Moorish-inspired menu. The punchy flavors can liven up an otherwise plain meat or fish dish.

MAKES 8 SMALL BOWLS OR 4 STARTERS

- 6 pita breads, cut into tiny pieces with scissors
- 3 tbsp extra-virgin olive oil
- 1 small head romaine or 2 baby gem lettuce, cut into small pieces
- 8 oz cherry tomatoes, halved
- 1 medium-sized cucumber, deseeded, or 3 Lebanese mini-cucumbers, finely diced
- 4 scallions, thinly sliced
- 1 red pepper, finely diced
- 6 radishes, thinly sliced

Small bunch fresh dill, chopped

Small bunch fresh mint, finely chopped

Salt and freshly ground black pepper

Pomegranate seeds, to garnish

DRESSING

- 1 small garlic clove, crushed
- ½ tsp each salt and pepper
- 1 tsp lemon juice
- 2 tsp red wine vinegar or pomegranate molasses
- ⅓ cup extra-virgin olive oil

PREPARATION TIME: 20 MINUTES

1. Preheat the oven to 400°F. Place the diced pita bread on a nonstick baking sheet, spoon on the olive oil, and turn to coat. Bake for about 5 minutes, turning once, until golden and crisp. Remove and leave to cool.

2. To make the dressing, put all the ingredients in a small glass jar, close the lid, and shake well until thoroughly mixed.

3. In a large bowl, combine the lettuce, tomatoes, cucumber, scallions, red pepper, radishes, herbs, and pitas.

4. Pour the dressing over the salad, season to taste with salt and pepper, and toss well. Divide between 8 small bowls or 4 appetizer plates. Sprinkle with pomegranate seeds, if using.

PREPARE AHEAD The pita chips can be baked and stored in an airtight container for 4 days. The dressing can be made the night before. The salad ingredients can be prepared about 4 hours in advance and kept covered in the refrigerator until ready to combine.

Five-Spice Hoisin Ribs with Scallions

Slow cooking makes the pork wonderfully tender, nearly to the point of melting off the bones. If you prefer, ask your butcher to prepare the spare ribs for you.

MAKES ABOUT 30 RIBS

3½ lb pork spare ribs, cut into single ribs and halved

  1 tsp five-spice powder

Salt and pepper

  5 scallions, finely sliced lengthwise, to garnish

SAUCE

  3 tbsp peanut oil

  2 tsp grated root ginger

  2 garlic cloves, crushed

¼ cup hoisin sauce

  2 tbsp soy sauce

  2 tbsp bottled sweet chili pepper dipping sauce

¼ cup honey

⅓ cup soft light brown sugar

⅓ cup dry sherry

PREPARATION TIME: 15 MINUTES; COOKING TIME: 2 HOURS

1. Preheat the oven to 275°F. Rub the ribs with the five-spice powder and season to taste with salt and pepper. Divide between 2 nonstick roasting pans, cover tightly with foil, and cook for 1 hour.

2. Meanwhile, to make the sauce, heat the oil in a wok over medium-high heat until hot and add the ginger and garlic. Fry for 1 minute, then add the remaining sauce ingredients. Remove the ribs from the oven and mix well with the sauce. Return to the oven and cook, covered, for 30 minutes. Remove the foil and complete cooking for a final 30 minutes. Serve on plates, garnished with the scallions.

Pea and Shrimp Samosas with Mango Chutney

Amchoor is dried ground mango and can be found in specialty and Indian food stores. If you can't find it, use lemon juice instead.

MAKES 20 SMALL SAMOSAS

- 1 large potato, about 8 oz
- 2 tbsp vegetable oil
- 1 small onion, finely chopped
- 1 garlic clove, chopped
- 1 tbsp fresh ginger, grated

Salt and pepper, to taste

1½ tsp each garam masala, cumin seeds, and amchoor

- 1 cup fresh or frozen peas

Small handful fresh cilantro, chopped, plus sprigs to garnish

- 8 jumbo shrimp, roughly chopped
- 20 gyoza or large spring roll wrappers
- 1 egg white, lightly beaten

2½ cups vegetable or peanut oil, for deep-frying

Bottled mango chutney, to serve

PREPARATION TIME: 20 MINUTES; COOKING TIME: 20 MINUTES

1. Peel the potato and cut it into chunks. Place the potato chunks in a saucepan of boiling, salted water and cook for 10 minutes or until soft. Mash roughly.

2. Meanwhile, heat the 2 tablespoons of vegetable oil in a frying pan over medium heat, add the onion, garlic, and ginger, and season with salt and pepper. Sauté for about 8 minutes, until soft. Add the garam masala, cumin seeds, and amchoor. Cook for a few minutes more, then add the potato, peas, and cilantro, mixing well. Remove from the heat and transfer to a small bowl. Stir in the raw shrimp.

joyce on alternatives to deep-frying

If you want to shave some calories off this dish, you can bake the samosas instead of frying them—just brush with oil and bake them in the oven. You can also shallow-fry them by using a small amount of oil in a wok.

3. Take the wrappers and place 2 tablespoons of the filling in each. Brush the edges with egg white and fold over to seal. If using spring roll wrappers, you will need to place the filling at one corner of the wrapper, then brush all the edges with egg white, and fold in from the filled corner.

4. Put the oil in a heavy-bottomed, medium-sized saucepan. Heat until a small piece of bread, dropped in, sizzles immediately. Fry 3–4 samosas for about 4 minutes, until crispy. Repeat with the other samosas. Drain on paper towels. Serve with the mango chutney and garnish with some cilantro sprigs.

PREPARE AHEAD The samosas can be made and refrigerated the night before. Alternatively, they can be placed in a single layer in an airtight container and frozen for 1 month. Thaw in the refrigerator before frying.

BEST OF THE BEST EXCLUSIVE

Vietnamese Chicken in Lettuce Parcels

4 SERVINGS

1 pound skinless, boneless chicken thighs, trimmed of visible fat and cut into 1½-inch pieces

3 tablespoons Asian fish sauce

3 small shallots, finely chopped

3 garlic cloves, minced

1 stalk of fresh lemongrass, tender white inner bulb only, minced

3 tablespoons finely chopped cilantro, plus ⅓ cup whole leaves for serving

1 tablespoon finely chopped mint, plus ⅓ cup whole leaves for serving

1½ teaspoons cornstarch

½ teaspoon kosher salt

¼ teaspoon freshly ground pepper

½ cup granulated sugar

1 head Boston or red leaf lettuce, leaves separated, large outer leaves discarded

1 small seedless cucumber—peeled, halved lengthwise and thinly sliced crosswise

1 small red onion, halved and thinly sliced

Asian chili paste, such as sambal or Sriracha for serving

1. Preheat the oven to 400°. Position a rack in the top third of the oven. In a food processor, pulse the chicken until coarsely ground; transfer to a bowl. Add the fish sauce, shallots, garlic, lemongrass, chopped cilantro and mint, cornstarch, salt and pepper and mix with your hands.

2. Line a large, rimmed baking sheet with parchment paper. Spread the sugar on a plate. Roll the chicken mixture into 1½-inch balls. Roll the balls in the sugar to coat. Transfer the chicken balls to the prepared baking sheet and bake for 15 minutes, until lightly browned and cooked through.

3. Meanwhile, arrange the lettuce, cilantro and mint leaves, cucumber and onion on a platter. Transfer the meatballs to a platter and serve with chili paste.

editor's note

Rolling these meatballs in sugar before cooking them might seem like an unconventional technique. However, it results in a sweet and sticky glaze that's wonderful with spicy chile paste and tangy Asian fish sauce.

Traditional ingredients for a Korean feast.

Eating Korean

by Cecilia Hae-Jin Lee

"I hate 'comprehensive' Asian cookbooks because they always leave out Korean food," says author Cecilia Hae-Jin Lee. Lee, who immigrated to the States at age seven in the late '70s, peppers *Eating Korean* with short essays that describe her life growing up in a food-obsessed Korean family. It's an intimate and affectionate perspective on a cuisine that can sometimes seem intimidating—with recipes ranging from classics like kimchi to modern adaptations like Seasoned Fried Chicken, Korea's answer to the Chicken McNugget.

Published by John Wiley & Sons, 272 pages, $27.50.

BEST RECIPES
Tofu Hot Pot
140

Kimchi Potato Pancakes
142

Seasoned Fried Chicken
143

**BEST OF THE BEST
EXCLUSIVE**
Kimchi Stuffing
145

Tofu Hot Pot

Soon Dubu

editor's note
Korean food is traditionally very spicy, and this Tofu Hot Pot is no exception. If you're sensitive to heat, we recommend adding the spice mix to the broth just a teaspoon at a time, tasting as you go.

Soon dubu is made from very soft, silky tofu, usually in a stone pot (*ddook baegi*). If you don't have a stone pot, a metal one will work fine but the presentation won't be the same. *Soon dubu* can be made with beef, seafood, kimchi, or really anything you'd like. It can be easily made into a vegetarian dish by using vegetable stock and adding things like Korean zucchini and onions instead of meat or seafood.

MAKES 2 TO 3 SERVINGS

- 4 teaspoons chili powder
- 2 garlic cloves, minced
- 2 teaspoons salt
- 2 teaspoons sesame oil
- 9 ounces soft tofu
- 6 clams
- 1 cup Beef Stock (recipe follows)
- 4 ounces squid, sliced into about 1-inch pieces
- 6 shrimp
- 2 green onions, cut into about 1-inch lengths
- 1 egg

1. In a small bowl, combine the chili powder, garlic, salt, and sesame oil. Set aside.

2. In a stone pot or other pot, add the tofu, clams, and 1 cup beef stock. Bring to a boil and add squid, shrimp, and seasoning. Let simmer another few minutes until the seafood is cooked. Add the green onions and cook for about another 1 to 2 minutes.

3. Serve bubbling hot with a raw egg to add to the broth immediately. Serve with rice and kimchi.

Beef Stock

Gogi Gookmul

Beef stock is used in beef-based Korean soups. Although some of the beef used to make the stock is often used in the soup itself, there is leftover beef in some cases.

MAKES ABOUT 12 CUPS

1 **pound beef brisket**

Water

In a large pot, boil the beef brisket in about 16 cups of water for approximately 2 to 3 hours over low heat, until stock has reduced about a fourth. Occasionally skim the foam and fat that rises to the top.

NOTE To skim fat, wait until the stock cools a bit. Then take a piece of cling wrap and place over the surface of the liquid. Discard and repeat until the fat is removed. Alternatively, refrigerate the stock until the fat congeals. Then remove and discard the fat.

Kimchi Potato Pancakes
Gamja Buchingae

lee on reheating
You can prepare these ahead of time and freeze or refrigerate them, but don't be tempted to microwave them. They're best reheated in a pan so they get nice and crispy.

These little pancakes are a cinch to make and yummy, too. Another great recipe to make with leftover kimchi, be sure to use traditional cabbage kimchi in any stage of fermentation, although the riper the better.

MAKES 4 PANCAKES

 1 pound potatoes, peeled and shredded

½ cup finely chopped kimchi, drained

 5 green onions, chopped

 1 egg

 1 tablespoon flour

 1 tablespoon salt

Vegetable oil for frying

 2 small red chile peppers, sliced into thin circles for garnish (optional)

A few sprigs of crown daisies (*soot*) for garnish (optional)

1. In a large bowl, add the potatoes, kimchi, green onions, egg, flour, and salt. Mix well until the potatoes are well coated.

2. In a large skillet or on a griddle, add just enough vegetable oil to thinly cover the surface, about 1 tablespoon at a time. Turn the heat to medium high. Take about ¼ of the batter and form into a ball. Flatten into a pancake, about ½ inch thick, and carefully place into the pan. Cook on one side until it turns golden brown and the potatoes are crispy around the edges (like hash browns). Flip and cook the other side. Adjust the heat as necessary to prevent burning, adding more oil as needed. Remove the pancake. Repeat with the remaining batter.

3. Cut the pancakes into 4 or 8 pieces. If you wish, garnish with a few slices of red pepper and/or a sprig of crown daisy in the middle.

Seasoned Fried Chicken

Yangnyum Dak

Fried chicken is not a traditional Korean dish. In fact, very few dishes are deep-fried in Korean cooking. After some discussion with my aunts, I decided to include this dish because it's an excellent example of how Koreans have incorporated Western fast food into their diet, but made it entirely their own. The chili paste adds a nice kick.

MAKES 4 TO 5 SERVINGS

About 1 pound chicken, small pieces (about 3 inches each)
½ onion, grated
1 egg
Water
1 cup cornstarch
1 teaspoon salt
1 teaspoon black pepper
Vegetable oil for frying
3 tablespoons chili paste
5 tablespoons sugar
4 tablespoons ketchup
1 teaspoon lemon juice

1. Marinate the chicken pieces in the grated onion for at least 30 minutes, but preferably an hour.

2. In a medium bowl, combine the egg, 1 cup of very cold water, cornstarch, salt, and black pepper. Mix just until moist; do not mix well.

3. In a saucepan, heat enough vegetable oil at about 350° to 365°F to immerse the pieces of chicken.

4. Dip the chicken pieces in the cornstarch mixture and carefully place in the hot vegetable oil, repeating until the pan is mostly full. Cook until the chicken is crispy and golden brown and is cooked through, about 10 minutes. To test if the pieces are cooked, remove the largest piece and cut into the thickest part to

lee on her favorite guilty treats

I adore ice cream; it's my favorite thing. In the mornings I hanker for ice cream—I'll even eat it for breakfast—but by midnight I'll be saying, "I gotta go get doughnuts."

the bone. The meat should be opaque throughout and the juices run clear. Remove the pieces and place on a plate lined with paper towels.

5. Repeat until all the pieces are cooked.

6. In a bowl, mix the chili paste, sugar, ketchup, and lemon juice. Add the chicken and mix until the pieces are well coated. Serve immediately with a side of pickled radishes or kimchi and rice.

BEST OF THE BEST EXCLUSIVE

Kimchi Stuffing

8 SERVINGS

One 12-ounce loaf rustic white bread, crust removed, bread cut into ½-inch cubes

5 tablespoons unsalted butter

3 celery ribs, chopped

3 garlic cloves, minced

1 medium onion, chopped

¾ cup kimchi, drained well and coarsely chopped

½ cup pecans, coarsely chopped

2½ teaspoons kosher salt

½ teaspoon dried oregano

½ teaspoon dried thyme

1 teaspoon freshly ground black pepper

2 large eggs, beaten

1¼ cups chicken stock or low-sodium broth

¼ cup fresh orange juice

1. Preheat the oven to 350°. On a large rimmed baking sheet, toast the bread cubes for 15 minutes, or until dry. Transfer to a large bowl.

2. In a large skillet, melt the butter. Add the celery, garlic and onion and cook over moderate heat until tender, about 8 minutes. Transfer to the bowl with the bread cubes. Add the kimchi, pecans, salt, oregano, thyme, pepper, eggs, chicken stock and orange juice; stir until the bread is evenly moistened. Transfer the stuffing to an 8-by-13-inch baking dish. Cover with foil and bake for 30 minutes. Turn the oven to broil and remove the foil. Broil the stuffing 3 inches from the heat for about 2 minutes, or until the top is browned and crisp. Serve hot.

MAKE AHEAD The unbaked stuffing can be refrigerated overnight. Bring to room temperature before baking.

editor's note

This stuffing is a Thanksgiving tradition for the Lee family. Lee calls it a "spicy sidekick" to the turkey. It combines classic American stuffing ingredients like bread cubes and herbs with kimchi, a spicy Korean condiment made from pickled cabbage and chiles.

Baked Eggs Rancheros, p. 148

Brunch

by Marc Meyer and Peter Meehan

Chef Marc Meyer was antibrunch when he opened Manhattan's Five Points restaurant seven years ago. When he finally caved in, he was determined to go beyond the basics—and Five Points became a sleeper hit. His new book contains his most popular recipes, many combining sweet and savory (the best thing about brunch): Rosemary Corn Scones and Baked Banana French Toast. Meyer points out that brunch is one of the easiest ways to entertain. These recipes might inspire you to try it.

Published by Universe Publishing, 176 pages, $24.95.

BEST RECIPES

Baked Eggs Rancheros
148

Creamy Cauliflower Soup
151

Rosemary Corn Scones
152

Baked Banana
French Toast
155

**BEST OF THE BEST
EXCLUSIVE**

Lemony Broccoli and
Chickpea Rigatoni
157

Find more recipes by
Marc Meyer at
foodandwine.com/meyer

Baked Eggs Rancheros

meyer on eggs

Every weekend we use about 150 dozen eggs at Five Points. They come from Keepsake Farms in upstate New York. I like buying from smaller producers even if I do pay about double what I'd pay for commercially raised eggs. I'm supporting someone in this area rather than a corporation and I know the eggs are fresh, extremely fresh, which is essential.

SERVES **4**

Grapeseed, corn, canola, or other neutral oil as needed

  4 whole corn tortillas plus 2 corn tortillas cut into matchsticks

  1 cup Salsa Verde (recipe follows)

12 large eggs

Salt and freshly ground black pepper

½ cup Crème Fraîche (purchased, or recipe follows)

  1 cup shredded sharp white Cheddar (about ¼ pound)

1½ to 2 cups Pico de Gallo (recipe follows)

1. Preheat the oven to 400 degrees. Bring at least 2 inches of oil to 375 degrees in a wide skillet. Add the whole tortillas to the oil a couple at a time; work in batches as necessary to avoid crowding the pan. Fry the tortillas about 4 minutes, flipping them once mid-fry, until crispy and golden. Remove the fried tortillas to a paper towel–lined sheet pan and let the oil return to temperature before you fry the next batch. Fry the tortillas cut into matchsticks last; they will crisp more quickly than the whole tortillas. You can complete this step 2 to 3 hours in advance and hold the fried tortillas at room temperature.

2. Lightly oil four ramekins or a 9-by-13-inch baking dish. Arrange the fried whole tortillas in the bottom of the dish(es) and spoon 3 to 4 tablespoons of Salsa Verde over them. Crack the eggs on top of the salsa, season with salt and pepper, drizzle a couple tablespoons of crème fraîche over the dish(es), and sprinkle with the Cheddar. Set the dish(es) on the lowest shelf of the oven and bake until the egg whites are just set and the yolks are still runny, about 12 to 15 minutes. Scatter the top with matchstick-cut fried tortillas, spoon the Pico de Gallo over all, and serve immediately.

Salsa Verde

MAKES 1 TO 1½ CUPS

¾ pound tomatillos, husked

1 small red onion, cut into ½-inch-thick slices

2 jalapeño chiles

1 poblano chile

A minimal amount of grapeseed, corn, canola, or other neutral oil

½ bunch cilantro, coarsely chopped

Salt

Juice of 1 lime

1. Preheat the broiler. Film the tomatillos, onion, jalapeños, and poblano very lightly with oil, tossing them in a large bowl or brushing on the oil with a pastry brush, and arrange them on a rimmed baking sheet. Set the sheet as close to the broiling element as possible and let the vegetables cook undisturbed until charred. Toss once and char the other side. Transfer the tomatillos and sliced onion to the work bowl of a food processor or blender.

2. Put the poblano and jalapeños in a plastic bag, or a small bowl with a plate or pot lid over it—the idea is to steam them with the residual heat from the charring process, loosening their skins and making them easier to peel. Peel the peppers (and seed them if you want a milder sauce) when they're cool enough to handle. Add them to the food processor or blender with the other charred ingredients.

3. Pulse the mixture a few times, then add the cilantro and process until almost pureed. Season with salt and lime juice, taste, and adjust as necessary. Use at once or store, covered, in the refrigerator for 3 or 4 days.

editor's note

Meyer recommends
adding shredded
carrots or diced ripe
avocado to any leftover
pico de gallo to make
a dip for tortilla chips.

Pico de Gallo

MAKES 1½ TO 2 CUPS

2 medium tomatoes, seeded and diced

1 small red onion, diced

1 jalapeño, seeded (or not, if you like it hot) and diced

½ bunch cilantro, chopped

Juice of 2 limes

Salt

1. Toss together the tomatoes, onion, jalapeño, and cilantro in a small bowl. Add lime juice and salt to taste. Use within a couple of hours.

Crème Fraîche

Today you can often find crème fraîche for sale in specialty stores, but making your own at home is easy and cheaper. Plus, making it at home allows for a less solid consistency that is better suited to this recipe. If you don't have crème fraîche or the time to make it, in most recipes you can just substitute heavy cream.

MAKES ABOUT 1 CUP

1 cup heavy cream

¼ cup buttermilk

1. Bring the cream to 98 degrees in a small saucepan over low heat (use an instant-read thermometer to check this), then remove it from the heat and let it sit for 5 minutes.

2. Add the buttermilk to the cream and whisk to incorporate. Let the mixture cool to room temperature and store it in the refrigerator overnight.

3. The crème fraîche will be ready in the morning and will be good for up to about 2 weeks (it will get increasingly tangy over the span of that time).

Creamy Cauliflower Soup

SERVES 4 TO 6

4 tablespoons unsalted butter

2 cloves garlic, roughly chopped

1 small yellow onion, roughly chopped

1 small dried chile

1 head cauliflower, roughly chopped

Salt and freshly ground black pepper

½ cup white wine

½ cup heavy cream

1 quart vegetable or chicken stock

editor's note

Meyer sometimes varies this recipe by adding a few anchovy fillets with the garlic or topping the soup with fried shallots and chopped herbs.

1. Heat the butter in a 4- to 6-quart saucepan over medium-high heat, and when the foam subsides, add the garlic. Cook, stirring frequently, until the garlic just begins to color, about 3 minutes. Add the onion and dried chile, lower the heat to medium, and cook, stirring occasionally, until the onion is golden and softened, about 10 minutes.

2. Add the cauliflower to the pan, toss it with the onion-garlic mixture, and sweat it for a few minutes, until the cauliflower begins to soften. Season with salt and pepper.

3. Turn the heat back to high and add the wine. Cook until reduced by half, about 5 minutes, then add the cream and enough vegetable or chicken stock to barely cover the cauliflower. Simmer for 20 minutes, until the stem pieces offer no resistance to the tip of a paring knife.

4. Puree the soup in a blender or pass it through a food mill. If the soup seems too thick, thin it to taste with additional stock, or use water or milk. At this point, you can store the soup in the refrigerator, tightly covered, for a day or two; hold it at room temperature for a couple hours and reheat it just before serving; or reheat it to serve immediately. Just before serving, check the seasoning. Serve hot.

Rosemary Corn Scones

A sweet/savory scone with a slight flavor of rosemary.

MAKES TWELVE 3-INCH-SQUARE SCONES

1½ cups (3 sticks) cold unsalted butter

3 cups all-purpose flour, plus additional for rolling out the dough

¾ cup cake flour

1¾ cups cornmeal

1 tablespoon plus ½ teaspoon baking powder

2 tablespoons stemmed and finely chopped fresh rosemary leaves, plus additional small sprigs for garnish

¾ cup light brown sugar

1 egg plus 1 egg yolk

2½ tablespoons honey

½ cup plus 2 tablespoons heavy cream

1 tablespoon melted butter

1 tablespoon turbinado sugar

1. Finely chop the cold butter and put it in the freezer for up to 15 minutes while you gather and measure out the rest of the ingredients. Preheat the oven to 400 degrees.

2. Combine the flours, cornmeal, baking powder, chopped rosemary, and brown sugar in the bowl of a food processor and pulse once to mix. Add the chopped, frozen butter and process it into the dry ingredients in short pulses until the butter is just incorporated into the flour, with a texture somewhere between sand and pebbles.

3. Add the egg and yolk, honey, and cream, and incorporate them in short, quick pulses, working the dough as little as possible. Turn the dough out onto a lightly floured board or counter, knead it gently for a few seconds to bring it together, and roll it out ¾-inch thick with a lightly floured rolling pin.

4. Cut scones out of the dough with a square cookie cutter (or cut them into 3-inch squares with a knife) and arrange them an inch apart on a parchment-lined baking sheet. Lightly knead the leftover dough back together, roll it out, and cut out more scones.

5. Brush the tops of the scones with the melted butter, dust them with turbinado sugar, and gently press a rosemary sprig into each one. Bake for 25 to 30 minutes, until golden brown and firm. Serve warm or at room temperature.

Baked Banana French Toast

SERVES 8

1 loaf Pullman brioche, crust removed

3 or 4 ripe bananas

1 tablespoon unsalted butter

1¼ to 1½ cups Crème Anglaise (recipe follows)

Water or milk

Maple syrup, warmed

1. Preheat the oven to 375 degrees. Cut the crustless loaf into eight 2½- to 3-inch-thick slices. Cut each slice diagonally into 2 triangles and cut a slit into the wide side of the wedge, creating a pocket.

2. Mash the bananas with a pestle, potato masher, or spoon if they're soft enough, until you have a nearly homogenous puree. You can put the mashed bananas into a pastry bag to pipe them into the wedges of bread (as we do at the restaurant) or fill the bread with a spoon. Stuff approximately 3 to 4 tablespoons of the bananas into each piece of bread, making sure they're generously filled but not overstuffed.

3. Lightly butter a sheet pan and put it in the oven (this step preheats the baking sheet). Thin the Crème Anglaise to a pourable consistency with a little water or milk if necessary, and pour it into a wide, shallow dish (a pie plate works great). Dip the stuffed bread into the thinned Crème Anglaise, lightly coating each side, gently shake off any excess, and arrange the prepared wedges on the sheet pan.

4. Bake for 12 to 15 minutes, until golden brown and mottled. You can serve the French toast immediately with maple syrup, or hold the wedges at room temperature for up to 4 hours. Reheat the stuffed French toast in a 350-degree oven until warmed through, about 5 minutes, before serving.

editor's note

Any high-quality unsliced bread (you need a loaf that weighs about 1½ pounds) will work for this French toast recipe, Meyer says. Even sourdough will be delicious.

Crème Anglaise

MAKES 1¼ TO 1½ CUPS

4 egg yolks
¼ cup sugar
Pinch of salt
2 teaspoons pure vanilla extract
1 cup heavy cream or half-and-half

1. Whisk together the egg yolks, sugar, salt, and vanilla in a small mixing bowl.

2. Warm the cream in a saucepan and, when it's hot to the touch (about 100 degrees), stir a few tablespoons of the warmed cream into the egg mixture to temper the eggs. Add the remainder of the cream to the eggs, whisking constantly, then pour the mixture back into the pan. Cook, stirring, over medium-low heat, until the sauce barely coats the back of a spoon.

3. Transfer the crème anglaise to a clean bowl (set in a larger bowl full of ice, if possible) and stir it until cool. Press a piece of plastic wrap against the surface of the cooled sauce to keep it from forming a skin and store in the refrigerator until you're ready to use it. The crème anglaise will keep in the fridge, covered, up to 2 days.

NOTE You may be skeptical about using crème anglaise as the batter for French toast, but its benefits are twofold: Not only is it richer and more flavorful than regular French toast batter, but it also buys you time. Because it is more stable, you can make the crème anglaise up to 2 days in advance, and bake the French toast up to 4 hours in advance.

BEST OF THE BEST EXCLUSIVE

Lemony Broccoli and Chickpea Rigatoni

4–6 SERVINGS

One 19-ounce can chickpeas, drained and rinsed

⅓ cup fresh lemon juice

¾ cup extra-virgin olive oil

Kosher salt and freshly ground pepper

1½ pounds broccoli, cut into florets

 1 pound rigatoni

 5 large garlic cloves, thinly sliced

½ teaspoon crushed red pepper

 1 cup freshly grated Parmesan cheese

1. In a medium bowl, toss the chickpeas with the lemon juice and ½ cup of the olive oil. Season with salt and pepper.

2. In a large pot of salted boiling water, cook the broccoli until crisp-tender, about 4 minutes. Using a slotted spoon, transfer the broccoli to a colander and rinse under cold water until cool. Add the rigatoni to the boiling water and cook until al dente.

3. Meanwhile, in a large, deep skillet, heat the remaining ¼ cup of olive oil. Add the garlic and crushed red pepper and cook over moderate heat until the garlic is golden, about 3 minutes. Add the broccoli and cook until tender, about 5 minutes. Add the chickpea mixture and cook until warmed through, about 1 minute.

4. Drain the rigatoni, reserving ¼ cup of the cooking water. Add the pasta to the broccoli and chickpeas along with the reserved cooking water and season with salt and pepper. Cook over moderate heat, stirring, until the rigatoni is coated with sauce. Remove from the heat and stir in ½ cup of the Parmesan cheese. Transfer the pasta to a bowl, sprinkle with the remaining Parmesan and serve.

editor's note

This quick and healthy pasta in a piquant lemon-Parmesan sauce (a favorite of Meyer's two teenage sons) epitomizes his unfussy, ingredient-centric style.

Rocky Recchiuti Brownies, p. 160

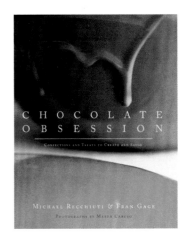

Chocolate Obsession

by Michael Recchiuti and Fran Gage

This lushly photographed book by Michael Recchiuti, owner of Recchiuti Confections in San Francisco, is the work of a master artisan. Recchiuti adroitly uses elements like caramelized sugar, jasmine tea and tarragon to add textures and flavors to his chocolates. Although some techniques are intimidating, numerous tips demystify them. The range of recipes is vast, from barks to drinks, but the go-to pages are in the snacks chapter, with recipes like Chocolate Shortbread Cookies with Truffle Cream Filling and Burnt Caramel Pots de Crème.

Published by Stewart, Tabori & Chang, 200 pages, $35.

BEST RECIPES

Rocky Recchiuti Brownies
160

White Cupcakes with
Truffle Cream Topping
163

Chocolate Shortbread
Cookies with
Truffle Cream Filling
167

Burnt Caramel
Pots de Crème
169

**BEST OF THE BEST
EXCLUSIVE**

Cocoa Nib Meringues
171

Find more recipes by
Michael Recchiuti at
foodandwine.com/recchiuti

Rocky Recchiuti Brownies

recchiuti on brownies

There are two different types of brownie people in the world: the cakey brownie people and the fudgy brownie people. I'm a fudgy brownie person; I like them kind of gooey. They should have a light, crackly surface that's almost like ice forming on water. When you touch it, it should break and not spring back.

16 BROWNIES

Flavorless vegetable oil for the pan

5½ ounces 100% unsweetened chocolate, coarsely chopped, divided

10 tablespoons (5 ounces) unsalted butter with 82% butterfat, cut into 1-inch slices

⅔ cup (3½ ounces) unbleached all-purpose flour

½ teaspoon kosher salt

3 (6 ounces) extra-large eggs, at room temperature

1 teaspoon pure vanilla extract, preferably Madagascar Bourbon

1⅓ cups (10 ounces) granulated cane sugar

⅓ cup (1½ ounces) walnut halves, roasted and roughly chopped

6 marshmallows, each 1½ inches square, cut into quarters

1. Preheat the oven to 325°F. Line the bottom of an 8-inch square baking pan with parchment paper and liberally coat the paper and the pan sides with flavorless vegetable oil.

2. Put 3 ounces of the chocolate and the butter in a medium stainless-steel bowl and set over a pot of simmering water. Heat, stirring occasionally, until the chocolate and butter melt and are fully combined and the mixture is smooth. Lift the bowl from the pot. Set aside.

3. Sift the flour and salt together into a bowl. In another bowl, combine the eggs and vanilla extract and whisk together by hand until blended. Whisk in the sugar.

4. Whisk the egg mixture into the chocolate. Add the flour and the remaining 2½ ounces chocolate to the batter and, using a rubber spatula, mix well. Then mix in the walnuts.

5. Pour the batter into the prepared pan. Spread it evenly with a small offset spatula. Scatter the marshmallow pieces evenly over the surface and push them halfway into the batter. The tops should remain uncovered.

6. Bake on the middle shelf of the oven until the marshmallows are browned and a skewer inserted into the center of the brownie sheet comes out with some batter clinging to it, about 45 minutes. Let cool completely in the pan on a wire rack, then cover with plastic wrap and refrigerate until cold.

7. Run a table knife around the edge of the pan to loosen the sides of the brownie, and then slide the brownie, still on the paper, onto a work surface. Using a ruler to guide you and a sharp knife, cut into sixteen 2-inch squares. Store in an airtight container in the refrigerator for up to 3 weeks.

White Cupcakes with Truffle Cream Topping

These tender cupcakes scented with vanilla are topped with a rich truffle filling, so chocolate lovers can have their cake and chocolate, too. The topping is a double recipe of the Truffle Cream Filling for the Chocolate Shortbread Cookies (page 167), but it is whipped to a fluffy lightness before being piped onto the cupcakes. These are best when served the same day they are made.

12 CUPCAKES

THE CUPCAKES

1½ cups (7½ ounces) unbleached all-purpose flour

1 teaspoon baking powder

½ teaspoon baking soda

¼ teaspoon kosher salt

1 cup (8 ounces) crème fraîche, at room temperature

2 (4 ounces) extra-large eggs, at room temperature

1 teaspoon pure vanilla extract, preferably Madagascar Bourbon

6 tablespoons (3 ounces) unsalted butter with 82% butterfat, at room temperature

¾ cup (5¼ ounces) granulated cane sugar

THE TOPPING

8 ounces 65% chocolate, coarsely chopped

⅔ cup (5 ounces) heavy whipping cream

⅔ cup plus 2 tablespoons (3 ounces) powdered cane sugar

4 tablespoons (2 ounces) unsalted butter with 82% butterfat, very soft (75°F)

1 tablespoon pure vanilla extract, preferably Madagascar Bourbon

BAKE THE CUPCAKES

1. Preheat the oven to 325°F. Line 12 standard muffin cups (2½ inches top diameter and 1¼ inches deep) with paper liners.

2. Sift the flour, baking powder, baking soda, and salt together into a medium bowl.

3. Combine the crème fraîche, eggs, and vanilla extract in a medium bowl and whisk by hand until well mixed.

4. Put the butter in the bowl of a stand mixer fitted with the paddle attachment. Beat on medium speed until the butter is creamy. Add the granulated sugar and beat until fluffy and pale.

5. Switch the mixer to low speed. Add the dry ingredients in 3 additions, alternating with the wet ingredients in 2 additions.

6. Using a tablespoon, divide the batter evenly among the muffin cups, filling them about two-thirds full.

7. Bake on the middle shelf of the oven until the cupcakes are puffed, lightly browned, slightly cracked on top, and a skewer inserted into the center of one comes out clean, 15 to 20 minutes. Let cool completely in the pan on a rack. When cool, remove the cupcakes, still in their paper liners, from the muffin cups.

MAKE THE TOPPING AND FINISH THE CUPCAKES

1. Put the chocolate in a medium bowl.

2. Put the cream and powdered sugar in a small saucepan and bring to a simmer over medium heat. Cook at a simmer for 1 minute and remove from the heat.

3. Pour the hot cream mixture over the chocolate. Whisk the mixture by hand until the chocolate melts. Whisk in the butter, and then the vanilla extract.

4. Pour into a bowl, cover with plastic wrap so that the wrap is touching the surface, and refrigerate until it is 70°F. This will probably take 30 to 40 minutes, but check after 20 minutes.

5. When the cream is at the correct temperature, put it into the bowl of the stand mixer fitted with the whip attachment. Beat on high speed until the mixture is lighter in color and less dense.

6. Put the topping into a pastry bag fitted with a ⅜-inch star tip. Pipe a swirl on the top center of each cupcake, distributing the topping evenly among them.

7. Store in a cool place until serving.

Chocolate Shortbread Cookies with Truffle Cream Filling

30 COOKIES

THE COOKIES

- 1 cup (5 ounces) unbleached all-purpose flour
- ⅓ cup plus 1 tablespoon (1½ ounces) unsweetened natural cocoa powder
- ⅛ teaspoon kosher salt
- 8 tablespoons (4 ounces) unsalted butter with 82% butterfat, at room temperature
- ½ cup (3½ ounces) granulated cane sugar
- ¼ teaspoon pure vanilla extract, preferably Madagascar Bourbon

THE FILLING

- 4 ounces 65% chocolate, roughly chopped
- ⅓ cup (2½ ounces) heavy whipping cream
- ⅓ cup plus 1 tablespoon (1½ ounces) powdered cane sugar
- 2 tablespoons (1 ounce) unsalted butter with 82% butterfat, very soft (75°F)

1½ teaspoons pure vanilla extract, preferably Madagascar Bourbon

Unsweetened natural cocoa powder for finishing cookies

MAKE THE DOUGH

1. Sift the flour, cocoa powder, and salt together into a bowl. Set aside.

2. Put the butter and sugar in the bowl of a stand mixer fitted with the paddle attachment. Beat on medium speed just until combined. Add the vanilla extract.

3. Switch the mixer to low speed and add the dry ingredients in 3 additions, pulsing the mixer to incorporate each addition before adding the next one. The dough will look dry.

4. Turn the dough out onto a lightly floured work surface. Knead a few times just until it comes together. Flatten into a disk, wrap in plastic wrap, and refrigerate until firm, at least 3 hours or up to 2 days.

editor's note

This recipe uses a slightly different technique for making shortbread dough. Usually recipes call for the butter and sugar to be creamed together until fluffy, but this method calls for beating these ingredients until just combined. Recchiuti explains that overmixing whips in excess air, resulting in cookies that spread too much in the oven.

BAKE THE COOKIES

1. Preheat the oven to 325°F. Line the bottoms of two 12-by-18-inch sheet pans with parchment paper.

2. Remove the dough from the refrigerator and unwrap it. On a lightly floured work surface, roll out the dough ⅛ inch thick. Using a 1½-inch round cookie cutter, cut out as many rounds as possible. Reroll the scraps only once, using less flour on the work surface to prevent toughness, and cut again. You should have 60 rounds in all. Place the rounds on the pans, spacing them ½ inch apart.

3. Bake on the middle shelves of the oven, rotating the pans 180 degrees halfway through the baking time, until the tops are lightly cracked and hold a slight indentation when pressed with a fingertip, about 10 minutes. Let cool completely on the pans on wire racks. Store in an airtight container at room temperature until you are ready to assemble the sandwiches.

MAKE THE FILLING AND ASSEMBLE THE COOKIES

1. Put the chocolate in a medium bowl. Put the cream and powdered sugar in a small saucepan and bring to a simmer over medium heat. Cook at a simmer for 1 minute and remove from the heat. Pour the hot cream mixture over the chocolate. Whisk the mixture by hand until the chocolate melts. Whisk the butter, and then the vanilla extract.

2. Pour the truffle cream into a bowl, cover with plastic wrap so that the wrap is touching the surface, and refrigerate until the consistency of thick mayonnaise, 30 to 45 minutes.

3. Arrange half of the cookies, bottom side up, on a sheet pan. Put the truffle cream into a pastry bag fitted with a ¼-inch star tip and pipe a swirl of the cream onto the top of each cookie, distributing the cream evenly among them. Top each covered cookie with a second cookie, bottom side down, and press gently to adhere it to the truffle cream. Store in a cool place until serving.

4. Just before serving, sift a dusting of cocoa powder on the tops of the cookies. Transfer to a serving plate.

Burnt Caramel Pots de Crème

Because a little of these rich custards goes a long way, bake them in espresso cups and bring them to the table to end a meal. They can be made a day ahead and refrigerated; allow them to come to room temperature before serving.

12 SERVINGS

- ¾ cup (5¼ ounces) granulated cane sugar
- 2 tablespoons (1 ounce) water
- ¾ cup (6 ounces) whole milk
- 2 cups (16 ounces) heavy whipping cream
- 5 (3¾ ounces) extra-large egg yolks
- 2½ ounces 41% milk chocolate, finely chopped

1. Put the sugar and water in a medium heavy-bottomed pot. Use an unlined copper pan if you have one. Stir to mix the water and sugar. Place over medium heat and cook, stirring occasionally with a wooden spoon, until the sugar melts. Then continue to cook, without stirring, until the sugar turns dark amber, 4 to 5 minutes. To check the color, dab a small amount of the syrup on a white plate. If any crystals form on the sides of the pan as the sugar darkens, wash them down with a wet pastry brush.

2. While the sugar is cooking, combine the milk and cream in a saucepan and bring to a boil over medium heat.

3. When the sugar is the correct shade, remove the pan from the heat and put a sieve or splatter guard over it. Wearing an oven mitt, slowly pour the hot cream into the sugar syrup a little at a time. The mixture will sputter and foam. Be careful, as it is very hot. When the mixture stops bubbling, whisk it to incorporate any caramel stuck to the bottom.

4. Place the egg yolks in a medium bowl and whisk by hand until blended. Whisk about ½ cup of the caramel mixture into the yolks to warm them gradually. Whisk in another 1 cup, and then whisk in the rest. Add the chocolate and whisk until it melts.

recchiuti on caramel

The one key factor with this recipe is that the sugar has to be burnt. Cook the sugar until it's almost carbonized—it's very close to being black— then add water to it to make a syrup.

Burnt Caramel Pots de Crème

5. Strain the custard through a fine-mesh sieve into a bowl. Spoon the custard into twelve 2½-ounce espresso cups, filling them three-fourths full. Let the custard cool to room temperature.

6. Preheat the oven to 300°F. Bring a large teakettle of water to a simmer.

7. Put the cups in a large baking pan. Pour the hot water into the baking pan to reach halfway up the sides of the cups. Cover the pan with aluminum foil.

8. Bake on the middle shelf of the oven until the tops are set but the entire custard jiggles when a cup is moved, about 25 minutes. Immediately remove the cups from the hot water. Let cool to room temperature.

9. Cover each cup and refrigerate for at least 6 hours or up to overnight. Bring to room temperature before serving.

BEST OF THE BEST EXCLUSIVE
Cocoa Nib Meringues

MAKES 4½ DOZEN 1½-INCH COOKIES

1½ cups cocoa nibs (6 ounces)

5 large egg whites

2 cups confectioners' sugar

1 vanilla bean, split, seeds scraped

1. Preheat the oven to 200°. Line 3 large baking sheets with parchment paper. In a food processor, pulse the cocoa nibs until coarsely ground. In a large saucepan, bring 2 inches of water to a simmer. In a large metal bowl, whisk the egg whites with the sugar, vanilla bean and seeds. Place the bowl over but not in the simmering water and whisk until the sugar is dissolved and the egg whites are thick enough to coat the back of a spoon, about 7 minutes. Remove the bowl from the heat and discard the vanilla bean.

2. Using an electric mixer, beat the egg whites at high speed, until stiff peaks form, about 3 minutes. Reduce the speed to medium and continue to beat until the meringue is cool, very stiff and glossy (about 5 minutes), then fold in the cocoa nibs.

3. Drop tablespoon-size mounds of the meringue onto the prepared baking sheets about 1½ inches apart. Bake for 1 hour and 15 minutes, or until the meringues are dry to the touch but still soft inside. Let cool on the baking sheets for 20 minutes.

MAKE AHEAD
The meringues can be stored in an airtight container for up to 2 days.

editor's note
Cocoa nibs are roasted pieces of cocoa bean that have been separated from their husks and broken into small pieces. They add a crunchy, subtle chocolate flavor (but no extra sweetness) to the meringues. They're available from specialty food stores or at scharffenberger.com.

Galatoire's in New Orleans,
a century-old French-
Creole institution.

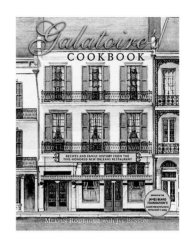

Galatoire's Cookbook

by Melvin Rodrigue with Jyl Benson

Although New Orleans's Galatoire's survived Hurricane Katrina relatively unscathed, it's impossible to look at this book without wondering about the restaurant's future and hoping the place will recover its uniquely buoyant spirit. Filled with photos depicting the well-heeled customers, the seen-it-all waiters and the plates of food at this 100-year-old French-Creole legend, Melvin Rodrigue and Jyl Benson's book captures the vibrant history of the place— as do recipes like Crabmeat au Gratin, Chicken Bonne Femme and Bread Pudding with Banana Sauce.

Published by Clarkson Potter, 272 pages, $35.

BEST RECIPES

Crabmeat au Gratin
174

Chicken Bonne Femme
176

Bread Pudding
with Banana Sauce
178

**BEST OF THE BEST
EXCLUSIVE**

Grilled Yellowfin
Tuna Provençal
179

Crabmeat au Gratin

rodrigue on new orleans

Stabilizing the city of New Orleans, that's what my calling is right now. I want to do everything I can for my sake, for my children's sake, for my fellow restaurateurs' sake. We've all got to get on the same page and bring the city back.

The use of gratin dishes is essential to the success of this recipe. The shallow dishes are either round or oval and allow for a great deal of surface area to be exposed to the heat from the broiler, ensuring a golden crispy topping for each portion.

Rich as this is, a simple green salad with vinaigrette and French bread complete the meal.

SERVES 4

2 tablespoons salted butter

¼ cup finely chopped scallions (white and green parts)

1 pound jump lump crabmeat, cleaned

1 cup Béchamel Sauce (recipe follows)

½ cup shredded mild Cheddar cheese

½ cup dried bread crumbs

½ cup Clarified Butter (recipe follows)

Preheat a broiler on low.

In a large sauté pan over high heat, melt the butter. Add the scallions and sauté for 2 minutes, or until tender. Add the crabmeat and sauté for an additional 3 minutes, or until the crabmeat is heated through. Reduce the heat to low and gently fold in the Béchamel Sauce and cheese, taking care not to break the lumps of crabmeat. Remove from the heat once the cheese is melted.

Spoon the mixture into 4 large gratin dishes. Sprinkle the tops with the bread crumbs and drizzle with the clarified butter, coating the bread crumbs. Place under the broiler until golden brown and serve immediately.

Béchamel Sauce

This recipe will yield a very thick version of the classic white sauce that serves as a base or additive for numerous French recipes. It is imperative to watch the roux carefully upon adding the flour. It will darken quickly. A blond roux is the desired result here. This Béchamel will keep for one week in the refrigerator.

MAKES 2½ CUPS

2 cups whole milk
1 cup (2 sticks) salted butter
½ cup all-purpose flour

In a medium saucepan, heat the milk until simmering. In a medium sauté pan, melt the butter and slowly incorporate the flour, whisking constantly over low heat to make a blond roux. Slowly incorporate 1 cup of the heated milk into the roux, whisking constantly. Cook over low heat for 10 minutes, until the mixture becomes paste-like in consistency. Slowly incorporate the remaining milk and whisk until smooth.

Clarified Butter

This will keep, sealed and refrigerated, for up to two weeks.

MAKES ABOUT 2 CUPS

1 pound salted butter

In a saucepan over low heat, melt the butter. Remove the pan from the heat and let the butter stand briefly. Skim the milk solids off the top and discard. Strain the butter to remove the remaining sediment. Reserve in a warm place until ready to use, or refrigerate for later use.

Chicken Bonne Femme

editor's note

If you don't want to go to the bother of deep-frying the potatoes in this recipe, try shallow-frying them in a skillet, in ¼- to ½-inch of oil.

In this case the "good woman" (*bonne femme*) is indulging in simple, hearty, delicious food. This classic French bistro dish is a meal in itself and would need only a simple green salad as an accompaniment, if anything at all.

SERVES 4

- ½ pound sliced bacon
- 1 fryer chicken, cut into 8 pieces
- Salt and freshly ground black pepper to taste
- Vegetable oil, for frying
- 4 tablespoons (½ stick) salted butter
- 2 large onions, julienned (about 4 cups)
- 1 tablespoon minced garlic
- 2 large Idaho potatoes, peeled and cut into ⅛-inch-thick slices
- ¼ cup chopped curly parsley, for garnish

Preheat the oven to 400°F.

Fry the bacon in a large sauté pan until crisp. Remove to a plate lined with paper towels while preparing the rest of the dish.

Rinse the chicken pieces and dry them thoroughly. Season the chicken generously with salt and pepper and bake on a rimmed baking sheet for approximately 30 minutes until golden brown, turning the pieces after 15 minutes.

While the chicken is baking, begin preparing the bonne femme garnish.

In a large, heavy-bottomed pot suitable for frying, heat the vegetable oil to 350°F.

In a separate large nonstick sauté pan over high heat, melt the butter. Add the onions and sauté for 8 to 10 minutes, until they start to become caramelized. Deglaze the pan with ½ cup of water to moisten the onions and lift any sugars that are on the bottom of the pan. Crumble the bacon into the onions and add the garlic to the hot pan. Toss to combine the ingredients, remove from the heat, and set aside.

Deep-fry the potatoes in the vegetable oil until they are golden brown. Remove them with a slotted spoon to drain on paper towels, and season with salt and pepper.

Toss the potatoes with the bacon and onions and set aside. This is the bonne femme garnish.

When the chicken is golden brown, divide the bonne femme atop the chicken pieces and bake together for an additional 3 minutes.

Divide the chicken bonne femme among 4 dinner plates. Finish the dish by sprinkling each portion with chopped parsley. Serve immediately.

Bread Pudding with Banana Sauce

editor's note

If you do not have an oversized muffin pan, Rodrigue and Benson recommend using one-cup ramekins or well-buttered baking dishes.

SERVES 12

11 large eggs

1⅓ cups granulated sugar

1 quart whole milk

1 teaspoon vanilla extract

1 teaspoon ground cinnamon

Twenty-four ¾-inch slices of French bread (baguettes)

1 pound salted butter

1 pound light brown sugar

4 bananas

½ cup praline liqueur

Preheat the oven to 350°F.

In a large mixing bowl, combine the eggs, granulated sugar, milk, vanilla, and cinnamon and whisk until well blended. In a nonstick oversized muffin pan (for 12) place 2 slices of the bread into the bottom of each muffin cup. Pour the egg and milk mixture into each muffin cup. Allow the bread to absorb the mixture and repeat the process until the bread is saturated and the muffin cup is full (it might take 3 or 4 fillings to totally saturate the bread and fill the cup). Bake the pudding mixture for 35 minutes, or until the pudding has turned golden and set in the pan.

While the pudding is in the oven, melt the butter in a 2-quart saucepan over medium heat. Add the light brown sugar and whisk over the heat until smooth. Slice the bananas, stir them into the sauce, and add the praline liqueur. Reduce the heat to low to keep the sauce warm.

When the pudding is baked, remove from the oven and allow it to sit for 15 minutes to cool. Invert the muffin pan to remove the puddings and expose the custard. Place each on the center of a plate and ladle the sauce onto the pudding. Serve immediately.

BEST OF THE BEST EXCLUSIVE

Grilled Yellowfin Tuna Provençal

4 SERVINGS

- 5 tablespoons salted butter
- 3 tablespoons extra-virgin olive oil
- 1 small onion, diced
- ¼ cup pitted French green olives, such as Picholine, halved lengthwise
- ¼ cup pitted Calamata olives, halved lengthwise
- 3 tablespoons capers, drained
- 3 garlic cloves, minced
- 3 cups grape tomatoes (1½ pints), halved
- 1 teaspoon thyme
- 1½ cups dry white wine
- One 6½-ounce jar marinated artichoke hearts, drained and rinsed
- 1 tablespoon fresh lemon juice
- Kosher salt and freshly ground pepper
- Four 6-ounce yellowfin tuna steaks, cut 1¼ inches thick

editor's note

This delicious, tangy tomato sauce is extremely versatile: Serve it with grilled or braised meat or pasta.

1. Light a grill. In a very large skillet, heat 2 tablespoons of the butter in 2 tablespoons of the olive oil. Add the onion and cook over moderately high heat until translucent, about 5 minutes. Add the olives, capers and garlic and cook for 1 minute. Add the tomatoes and thyme and cook, stirring occasionally, until the tomatoes begin to soften, about 4 minutes. Add the wine and cook over high heat until reduced by half, about 5 minutes. Stir in the artichoke hearts, lemon juice and the remaining 3 tablespoons of butter and season with salt and pepper. Cover and keep warm.

2. Brush the tuna steaks with the remaining 1 tablespoon of olive oil and season on both sides with salt and pepper. Grill the tuna over moderately high heat, turning once, until the steaks are lightly browned on the outside and pink in the center, about 5 minutes. Spoon the sauce onto plates, top with the tuna steaks and serve.

Dining on the veranda,
Southern style.

Seasoned in the South

by Bill Smith

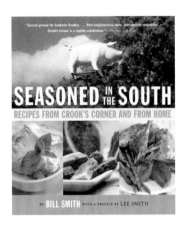

Bill Smith's first cookbook offers terrific recipes—and disarming directness. As Smith, the chef for over a decade at Crook's Corner in Chapel Hill, North Carolina, writes, "I prefer meals that are to be eaten and not dissected at the table." For him that means a kind of modern down-home cooking that fuses French technique with Southern ingredients—as in a summery Green Peach Salad or a spicy Green Tabasco Chicken.

Published by Algonquin Books of Chapel Hill, 208 pages, $19.95.

Green Peach Salad

smith on green peach salad

If you have any leftover salad you can use it as a relish. I like to pair it with pork dishes or serve it with cold meats and paté.

Sometimes you end up with unripe peaches despite your best efforts, especially if you buy a whole bushel. This is a wonderful way to use some of them. It is great with cold meats.

SERVES 4–6

2½ pounds of unripe peaches, peeled and sliced as for a pie

Scant ¼ cup sugar

½ teaspoon salt

½ teaspoon freshly ground black pepper

2 tablespoons strong-flavored extra-virgin olive oil, like Greek or Lebanese

2 tablespoons fresh mint chiffonade

Toss the peaches with the sugar and the salt. Let them sit for 10 minutes. Fold in the pepper, oil, and mint. Serve cold within a few hours of preparation, as it will become mushy overnight.

Skillet Eggplant

This recipe was given to me by a friend of a friend at a covered-dish dinner years ago and I promptly lost it. Then, miraculously, it fluttered unaltered out of an old notebook when I was looking for something else. I use this as a main course, but it would be a great addition to one of those summer buffet suppers when "we're eating out of the garden tonight."

When I tasted this at the party, I complimented the cook, who told me that it was a dish that his grandmother made often. When I asked if his grandmother was an Italian, he replied, "No, she's an old lady from Asheville."

SERVES 4–6

  2 pounds eggplant, peeled and cut into 1-inch cubes (about 6 cups)

1½ teaspoons salt

  1 medium onion, peeled and cut into large dice (about 1 cup)

¼ cup extra-virgin olive oil

1½ tablespoons (packed) light brown sugar

¼ cup balsamic or sherry vinegar

½ to 1 cup water

¾ cup large stuffed green olives, drained

½ teaspoon freshly ground black pepper

  1 cup feta cheese, coarsely crumbled, or a ball of fresh mozzarella, cubed

Dust the eggplant with salt and place in a colander to sweat for 20 minutes. Sauté the onion in a large skillet in the oil until it begins to soften and brown slightly. Shake off the eggplant and add to the onion, in batches if necessary, as it cooks down. Don't worry about the salt. Add the brown sugar, then the vinegar, and then enough water (start with ½ cup) to lubricate the stew. Cover and simmer for 15 minutes. Stir in the olives and warm through, about 3 minutes. Add the pepper and, if necessary, the rest of the salt. Lastly, fold in the cheese. After you have made this once, you may want to adjust the amounts of sugar or vinegar to match your idea of sweet and sour.

Green Tabasco Chicken

My friend Sara Hutt was living at my house the summer she studied for the bar. We had a small backyard garden and one of our most successful crops was hot chiles. We put up many bottles in vinegar. These vinegars became extremely hot. Mine sat in the refrigerator for months. By then Sara was living in Washington. In a phone conversation she mentioned that she had been marinating whole chickens in the vinegar before roasting them and that the results were delicious and surprisingly mild. Several years later the Tabasco company introduced a new product: Tabasco Green Pepper Sauce. This stuff is so delicious that I could drink it. I remembered Sara's recipe and adapted it thusly.

SERVES 4–6

- 1 whole chicken (about 3 pounds), well rinsed and patted dry
- 1 teaspoon salt
- ½ teaspoon freshly ground black pepper
- 1 lemon
- 1 jalapeño
- 1 clove garlic, peeled
- 1 bottle Tabasco Green Pepper Sauce or other green hot pepper sauce

Melted butter or bacon grease, for basting

1½ cups of dry white wine

Preheat the oven to 500° F. Snip off the pope's nose (see Note) and the last joint of each of the chicken's wings. Salt and pepper the cavity and stuff it with the lemon, jalapeño, and garlic. Truss up the chicken with kitchen twine and place it on a rack in a roasting pan. Baste the chicken with a half a bottle of the Tabasco. Sprinkle salt and lots of black pepper on the wet Tabasco. Place the chicken in the oven.

Put the trimmings plus the giblets of the chicken, minus the liver, in a 1-quart saucepan and cover with cold water. Bring to a simmer and let it cook while the chicken roasts. This will be the base for the sauce.

In about 20 minutes you should begin to hear the chicken sizzling. When you do, reduce the heat to 350°F and baste the chicken with the butter or bacon grease. Repeat every 20 minutes. Cook until the legs can be wiggled easily. This should take between 1 and 1¼ hours. I prefer roasted chicken to be a little past done; it will be better cold the next day, if there is any left.

Let the chicken rest for 20 minutes on the counter. If it is then cool enough to handle, remove the string. Use poultry shears (if you cook chickens a lot, you really should buy these) to cut out the spine. Try to save all the juice that will be in the cavity. Put the juice, spine, jalapeño, and garlic into the sauce pot and turn up the heat to a heavy boil, but discard the lemon, as it will make the sauce bitter.

Place the roasting pan on top of the stove and turn the eye up high. Pour the wine onto it and use a metal spatula to scrape up all of the browned bits and drippings. Add all this to the sauce. Let it reduce until it begins to thicken. The time will vary according to the amount of liquid you begin with. Degrease.

Cut the chicken into serving pieces and arrange on a platter. When the sauce has reduced until it is thick and lustrous, strain it through a sieve over the chicken. If there is more sauce than the platter can hold, bring the rest to the table in a sauceboat.

We serve this with mashed potatoes and wilted spinach.

NOTE The term *pope's nose* is used to refer to the tail of the chicken at one end of the spine. My very Catholic great-grandmother was fond of it (and bone marrow and pig knuckles, etc.). When she would use the term in polite company, my grandmother Annie and my aunt Theresa would roll their eyes heavenward and say, "Oh Mother, honestly!"

smith on green tabasco chicken

Tabasco Green Pepper Sauce was quite a revelation to me. I think it's delicious! My mother makes this recipe all the time, my sisters make it all the time, I have people come up to me constantly and say, "I love that." This chicken recipe is the easiest thing it could possibly be, which is the whole point of the cookbook as far as I'm concerned.

Cashew Cake with Madame Constance's Maple Frosting

smith on syrup

With this recipe we use Grade B maple syrup because Grade A is expensive and you don't need it— and it does make a difference in cost.

If you are ever invited to my house for dinner, some form of this cake will likely be your dessert. I rarely have time to entertain at home, so I like to make something familiar and quick. This recipe calls for cashews, but I have used pecans, almonds, pistachios, and hazelnuts. I have iced it with lemon curd, whipped cream, and in this instance a sort of buttercream made from maple syrup, a recipe I learned years ago in Quebec from a wonderful cook.

Madame Constance was the housemother of a remote youth hostel on the northeastern shore of the St. Lawrence River at Sault-au-Mouton. She had another maple sugar trick that I have never quite been able to duplicate. She served hot blueberry cobbler. On top she first put vanilla ice cream. Then she poured ice cold heavy cream. *Then* she immediately poured boiling hot maple sugar over the whole thing, creating a sort of web of taffy all over the cobbler. I've never forgotten it.

SERVES 8–10

  2 tablespoons (¼ stick) unsalted butter, softened to room temperature
1½ pounds raw cashews
  3 cups sugar
Zest of 1 large orange
  2 teaspoons cider vinegar
  1 teaspoon salt
  2 cups egg whites (about 16 eggs, with yolks reserved for frosting)
  ¼ teaspoon cream of tartar
  ¾ cup sifted all-purpose flour, plus more for tossing nuts
Madame Constance's Maple Frosting (recipe follows)

Preheat oven to 350° F. Butter two 9-inch springform pans, line them with parchment, and butter and flour the parchment.

Grind the cashews coarsely with half of the sugar and the orange zest in a food processor. Cashews are very oily, so beware that they are not ground so far as to begin to form a paste. Toss with a bit of flour to help keep the nut meal separate.

Rinse a mixing bowl with the vinegar. Swirl in the salt. Shake the bowl over the sink, but don't wipe it out. In it, beat the egg whites with the cream of tartar and then the rest of the sugar. Beat until soft peaks form. Fold the egg whites into the nuts by thirds, and with the last third gently include the sifted flour. Divide the batter between the two cake pans.

Bake for about 1 hour. The cake should be pretty and brown and a toothpick or broom straw should come out clean when inserted at the center. Allow to cool on racks for at least 1 hour before removing the springforms.

Each cake will be a layer. The cakes must be absolutely cool before they can be iced or the icing will spoil.

Madame Constance's Maple Frosting

This will be a cinch if you have ever made buttercream icing. You will need an electric mixer.

2 CUPS OF FROSTING, ENOUGH FOR A TWO-LAYER CAKE

- 8 large egg yolks
- ¾ cup sugar
- ½ cup Grade B pure maple syrup
- 1 pound unsalted butter, cut into small bits and softened

Beat the egg yolks with the whisk attachment of an electric mixer for 10 minutes or so on high until they have become pale yellow. Combine the sugar and the maple syrup in a saucepan and bring them to a boil that can't be stirred down, about 3 minutes.

Reduce the mixer speed to medium and slowly drizzle the maple syrup in a thin stream into the egg yolks. Aim so that you don't hit the whisk and sling the hot sugar out into the room. Add all the syrup. Turn off the mixer and scrape down the bowl with a spatula. Return the mixer to high speed. The egg yolks will be fairly hot, so beat the mixture until it has cooled back down to room temperature. Don't cheat. The eggs must be cool enough so that the butter does not melt

**smith on
becoming a chef**
I learned on the job.
It never actually
occurred to me to be a
chef. It just turned
out that it was a
good match once I
discovered it.

when added to them. When the side of the mixing bowl feels cool, add the butter, bit by bit, until it is all absorbed.

This recipe will make enough frosting to put between the layers and to ice the outside of the two cashew layers. Needless to say, this is very sweet, so sometimes I put barely sweetened whipped cream between the layers and on top of the cake and only use the frosting on the sides. The extra frosting will refrigerate fairly well for a week if tightly wrapped in plastic. It must be softened very slowly at room temperature and applied with a warm knife or spatula.

BEST OF THE BEST EXCLUSIVE

Deviled Eggs

8 SERVINGS

- 1 dozen large eggs
- 2 tablespoons yellow mustard
- 1 tablespoon mayonnaise
- 1 tablespoon apple cider vinegar
- 2 small jalapeños, seeded and minced
- ⅓ cup minced red onion
- 2 tablespoons seeded and minced cucumber
- 2 tablespoons minced celery

Kosher salt and freshly ground pepper

Paprika, for dusting

1. In a large saucepan, cover the eggs with cold water and bring to a boil over high heat. Cover, remove from the heat and let stand for 14 minutes. Drain the eggs and cool them under cold running water. Add ice cubes to the saucepan and let stand until the eggs are completely cool. Drain and peel the eggs.

2. Halve the eggs lengthwise. Gently remove the yolks and transfer them to a medium bowl. Mash lightly with the back of a fork. Stir in the mustard, mayonnaise and vinegar. Gently fold in the jalapeños, onion, cucumber and celery. Season with salt and pepper.

3. Arrange the egg white halves cut-side up on a serving plate. Using a teaspoon, generously fill the cavities with the yolk mixture. Sprinkle with the paprika and serve.

editor's note

Smith doesn't really care for eggs, but he loves this spicy hors d'oeuvre. His version of this retro dish includes lots of crunchy vegetables, jalapeño peppers and a tangy bite of mustard. Smith's recipe calls for a good amount of jalapeño, but if you're sensitive to heat, then just add it to taste. If you like spicy food, Smith advises leaving in the jalapeño seeds.

A country kitchen like this one would be a dreamy place to try a recipe from *The Rustic Table*.

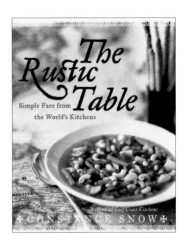

The Rustic Table

by Constance Snow

"I like no-nonsense cooking," writes author Constance Snow. "So this book is for cooks who enjoy adventure within reason, who want to re-create authentic cuisine but don't have time to make tortillas from scratch or hunt down yuzu rind." Snow, the award-winning author of *Gulf Coast Kitchens,* dedicates her latest book to hunting out great "peasant food" — straightforward and satisfying. "Rustic food is colorful and vibrant," she explains, " and that's because, for a lot of people, food is one of the only real pleasures that they have in life." A great tribute to unsung food traditions around the world.

Published by William Morrow, 368 pages, $24.95.

Greek-Style Orzo and Shrimp Salad

Orzo is rice-shaped pasta that is available in most supermarkets; it's fine to use small shells or another pasta shape. If you prefer, substitute cooked chicken or chickpeas for the shrimp.

SERVES 6 AS A ONE-BOWL MEAL, 8 TO 12 AS A STARTER OR SIDE

Salt

- 1 pound dry orzo or small pasta shells
- 4 garlic cloves
- 2 tablespoons fresh lemon juice
- 1 teaspoon fresh thyme leaves, or ¼ teaspoon dried
- ¼ cup olive oil
- 1 pound cooked and cleaned shrimp
- 3 fresh tomatoes, seeded and chopped
- 1 small cucumber, peeled, seeded, and chopped
- ¼ pound feta cheese, crumbled
- 2 tablespoons minced fresh mint
- 2 tablespoons minced fresh parsley

Freshly ground black pepper

Oil-cured black olives

1. Bring a large pot of salted water to a boil, add the orzo and garlic cloves, and cook until the pasta is al dente, 9 to 11 minutes. Drain and rinse with cool water; then drain again.

2. Mash the cooked garlic with ¼ teaspoon salt in a serving bowl. Whisk in the lemon juice, thyme, and olive oil. Add the orzo, shrimp, tomatoes, cucumber, feta, mint, and parsley; toss well. Taste, and add more salt if needed. Season with black pepper. Serve at room temperature, garnished with black olives.

PLAN AHEAD Refrigerate the completed salad for several hours. Let it return to room temperature before serving.

Mom's Macaroni-and-Cheese Custard

This is the way my mom made it, old New Orleans style. As for the appropriate vessel, there are two schools of thought: If you like plenty of brown and crusty edges, bake it in a shallow oblong pan. If you prefer tall custardy wedges, use a well-greased round casserole (or even a springform pan) and cut it into wedges like a cake. Colby cheese has a mild flavor and a pleasantly stretchy texture that works especially well here.

editor's note
This recipe calls for Colby or mild Cheddar, but if you like a more pronounced cheese flavor, sharp Cheddar works just as well.

SERVES 6 TO 8 AS A MAIN COURSE, 10 TO 12 AS A SIDE

Salt
 1 pound dry elbow macaroni
Butter or nonstick cooking spray for the baking dish
 ½ to ¾ pound Colby or mild Cheddar cheese, cubed
 6 large eggs
1 to 2 tablespoons sugar, optional
 3 cups milk
 ¼ teaspoon grated nutmeg
 ¼ teaspoon white pepper, or to taste

1. Preheat the oven to 350°F.

2. Bring a large pot of salted water to a boil, add the macaroni, and cook until al dente, 6 to 8 minutes (don't overcook); then drain it well.

3. Butter a large baking dish or deep casserole. Toss the macaroni and the cheese cubes together in the baking dish.

4. Beat the eggs with the sugar, if using, in a mixing bowl. Stir in the milk, nutmeg, and pepper. Add salt to taste, remembering that the cheese will be rather salty. Pour the custard mixture over the macaroni and cheese, and bake for 40 to 50 minutes (in a shallow baking dish) or 50 to 60 minutes (in a deep casserole). Serve hot.

Corn and Tomato Salad with Fried Okra Croutons

snow on family tradition
I come from a big French-Creole family and everybody cooks. That's the seat of power in our house: Whoever's in charge of the meal is in charge of everything for the day.

SERVES 4 AS A ONE-BOWL MEAL, 6 AS A STARTER OR SIDE

Southerners are known for their ability to turn a blind eye to the unpleasantries of life, so if something seems too ugly and slimy to eat, we just ignore the baser aspects, cover it with cornmeal, and throw it into a sizzling iron skillet. Thus okra, one of nature's most imperfect foods, is transformed into ethereal little crisps that even a Yankee could love. Good old "fried okry" is great on its own (as a traditional side dish or offbeat cocktail snack), but it also adds an extra layer of texture and flavor to the simplest garden salads. Here fresh sweet corn and vine-ripened tomatoes are essential, so save this one for a cool meal in midsummer, when the vegetables are at their best.

SALAD

Kernels from 4 ears fresh yellow or white corn, about 4 cups

- 2 large ripe tomatoes, seeded and chopped
- 2 thin scallions (white and green parts), thinly sliced
- 2 tablespoons minced fresh flat-leaf parsley
- ½ teaspoon sugar

Salt

- 2 teaspoons cider vinegar
- 2 tablespoons extra virgin olive oil
- ½ teaspoon fresh thyme leaves, or a pinch of dried

Freshly ground black pepper

FRIED OKRA

- ½ cup yellow cornmeal
- 1 teaspoon salt

Freshly ground black pepper

- 1 pound fresh okra, cut into ¼-inch rounds

Peanut or canola oil

1. Place the corn kernels in a microwave-safe bowl, and microwave on high power for 1 minute; stir, and microwave just until crisp-tender, up to 1 minute longer. (Alternatively, steam the corn in a vegetable steamer for 1 to 2 minutes.) Toss the corn in a mixing bowl with the tomatoes, scallions, and parsley.

2. Whisk the sugar and ¼ teaspoon salt with the vinegar in a small bowl until dissolved. Then whisk in the olive oil and thyme leaves until the dressing is thick and well blended. Pour the dressing over the salad, tossing to coat it well. Season with pepper, and additional salt if needed. Set the salad aside to allow the flavors to mellow while you fry the okra.

3. Combine the cornmeal, salt, and pepper to taste in a bowl, and toss the okra slices in the mixture. Warm ¼ inch of oil in a large skillet, preferably cast iron, over medium-high heat.

4. Drop a cornmeal-coated okra slice into the hot oil to test the temperature. When it sizzles energetically, add half of the remaining okra slices, without crowding. Fry until very crisp and lightly browned, about 5 minutes. Remove them with a slotted spatula and place them on paper towels to drain. Repeat with the second batch.

5. Just before serving, taste the salad and adjust the seasonings if needed. Top each dish of salad with a generous mound of fried okra.

Normandy Chicken and Apple Sauté

SERVES 4

Normandy, the great apple-growing region of France, is also the source of the dry apple brandy known as Calvados. Although imports can be pricey in the U.S. and some grand versions are aged for decades, Calvados is traditionally a drink of the common man, often used for cooking. Here you might substitute domestic applejack or hard cider. Serve this rich autumn supper with toasted French bread, steamed butternut squash, and a salad of mixed greens tossed with a garlicky vinaigrette.

4 tablespoons (½ stick) unsalted butter
One 3-pound frying chicken, cut into 8 pieces
Salt and white pepper
3 cooking apples (such as Granny Smith or underripe Golden Delicious), unpeeled, cored, and cut into 8 wedges each
1 large onion, halved lengthwise and sliced into thin wedges
1 cup chicken stock, preferably homemade (recipe follows)
¼ cup Calvados
½ cup heavy cream
½ cup coarsely chopped toasted walnuts

1. Heat 2 tablespoons of the butter in a large nonstick skillet over medium-high heat. Season the chicken pieces with salt and white pepper, and brown them evenly on all sides (in batches if necessary), 7 to 10 minutes. Remove the chicken from the skillet.

2. Sauté the apple wedges in the pan drippings until crisp-tender, about 3 minutes. Remove and reserve the apples.

3. Add the remaining 2 tablespoons butter to the pan drippings and sauté the onion until just golden, 2 to 3 minutes. Return the chicken pieces to the skillet, and add the stock and Calvados. Bring just to a boil; then cover the pan, reduce the heat to low, and simmer for 20 minutes. Add the apple wedges and continue simmering until they're heated through, 1 to 2 minutes.

4. Strain and reserve the cooking liquid. Arrange the chicken, onions, and apples on a warmed serving platter; cover it to keep warm. Return the cooking liquid to the skillet, add the cream, and bring to a gentle boil over medium heat. Continue cooking until thick, 2 to 3 minutes. Taste, and adjust the salt and pepper if needed. Spoon the sauce over the chicken; then sprinkle on the walnuts and serve immediately.

Chicken Stock

MAKES 4 QUARTS

- 4 pounds chicken parts or bones, or the carcass from a roasted turkey
- 2 garlic cloves, unpeeled and quartered
- 2 carrots, coarsely chopped
- 1 celery rib with leaves, coarsely chopped
- 1 onion, unpeeled and quartered
- 6 flat-leaf parsley sprigs
- 2 thyme sprigs, or ¼ teaspoon dried thyme
- 1 bay leaf
- ½ teaspoon black peppercorns
- 4 quarts water

Salt, optional

Place all the ingredients except the salt in a large stockpot, and bring just to a boil. Reduce the heat and simmer gently, uncovered, skimming the surface as needed to remove impurities, for 2 hours. Strain, pressing on the solids to extract as much flavor as possible, and discard the solids; degrease. Add salt if desired.

Warm Peach Shortcake with Brandy Whipped Cream

editor's note

This recipe is Snow's riff on a Southern shortcake—she makes one giant shortcake, splits it and fills it with warm, buttery peaches. To serve, she cuts it in wedges and tops each piece with brandy-laced whipped cream.

8 SERVINGS

SHORTCAKE

½ cup plus 1 tablespoon sugar

¼ teaspoon ground cinnamon

2 cups all-purpose flour

2 teaspoons baking powder

½ teaspoon freshly grated nutmeg

½ teaspoon salt

¼ teaspoon baking soda

1 stick (4 ounces) cold unsalted butter, cut into ½-inch pieces, plus 1 tablespoon unsalted butter, melted

¾ cup buttermilk

2 large eggs, beaten

FILLING

3 tablespoons brandy

¼ cup golden raisins

3 tablespoons unsalted butter

4 firm, ripe peaches (1½ pounds)—halved, pitted and sliced ½ inch thick

½ cup packed light brown sugar

¼ teaspoon ground cinnamon

1 cup heavy cream

1. Make the shortcake: Preheat the oven to 375°. Spray a 9-inch cake pan with nonstick vegetable spray. In a small bowl, stir 1 tablespoon of the sugar with the cinnamon. In a large bowl, whisk the flour with the remaining ½ cup of sugar, the baking powder, nutmeg, salt and baking soda. Using a pastry blender or 2 knives, cut in the cold butter until it is the size of small peas. Make a well in the center and add the buttermilk and the beaten eggs. Stir with a fork, until a dough forms. Scrape the dough into the prepared cake pan and bake for 35 minutes, until the top is golden. Brush the top of the hot cake with the melted butter and sprinkle with the cinnamon-sugar. Transfer the shortcake to a rack to cool for 10 minutes.

2. Meanwhile, make the filling: In a small bowl, pour the brandy over the raisins and let stand for 20 minutes. In a large skillet, melt the butter. Add the peaches, cover and cook over moderately low heat until the peaches just begin to soften, about 6 minutes. Reserve 1 tablespoon of the brandy. Add the remaining brandy and the raisins to the skillet along with the brown sugar and cinnamon. Cook the peaches over moderate heat, stirring often, until glazed and crisp-tender, about 8 minutes.

3. In a medium bowl, whip the cream with the reserved 1 tablespoon of brandy until soft peaks form. Remove the shortcake from the pan and transfer to a serving plate or cake stand. Using a serrated knife, slice the cake in half horizontally; slide the top of the cake onto a plate. Spoon the peaches and their sauce over the bottom of the shortcake. Top with the other half of the cake. Cut the shortcake into wedges and serve with a dollop of brandy whipped cream.

MAKE AHEAD The shortcake can be baked up to 1 day ahead and kept at room temperature.

Peanut Noodles with Mango, p. 202

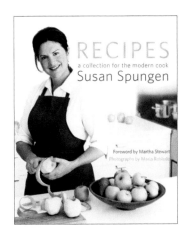

Recipes

by Susan Spungen

"The recipes in this book are my repertoire. They are the dishes that I come back to again and again," says Susan Spungen, founding food editor of *Martha Stewart Living.* "I wanted people to open the book and find what they're craving on any particular day." *Recipes* is organized by technique, starting with the basics in chapters like "Prepare" and "Chop," then moving on to "Sauté," "Roast" and "Grill." Nearly every recipe is accompanied by a picture—invariably beautiful.

Published by William Morrow, 288 pages, $34.95.

Find more recipes by
Susan Spungen at
foodandwine.com/spungen

Peanut Noodles with Mango

editor's note

Be sure to rinse the noodles thoroughly with cold water after cooking and before tossing them with the peanut dressing. If you don't, the noodles can easily end up gloopy.

These noodles are the perfect thing to bring to or serve at a summer party. They can be made hours, even a day, ahead of time and they won't become gummy. Mango, while an unorthodox addition, adds juiciness and bright color. Sugar snap peas provide crunch, but don't add them until serving time.

SERVES 8 TO 10 AS A SIDE DISH

FOR THE PEANUT DRESSING

- ¾ cup smooth natural-style peanut butter
- 3 tablespoons rice vinegar
- ¼ cup plus 2 tablespoons low-sodium soy sauce
- 4 tablespoons dark sesame oil
- 1 heaping tablespoon grated ginger

Scant teaspoon red pepper flakes

- ¾ teaspoon sugar

FOR THE NOODLE SALAD

Kosher salt

- 1 pound thick spaghetti
- 2 cups sugar snap peas, strings removed, or snow peas
- 2 ripe mangos

Juice of 1 lime

- 2 scallions, thinly sliced
- ½ cup loosely packed cilantro leaves, coarsely chopped
- ¼ cup roasted peanuts

1. Make the peanut dressing by combining the peanut butter, vinegar, soy sauce, oil, ginger, red pepper flakes, sugar, and ½ cup hot water in a mini food processor. Blend well and set aside. (This can be made several days ahead of time.) Store in an airtight container in the refrigerator.

2. Bring a large pot of water to a boil. Add 1 tablespoon salt and the spaghetti and cook according to package directions, stirring occasionally, until al dente.

3. Meanwhile, bring a small saucepan of water to a boil. Cook the peas until they turn bright green, about 30 seconds. Drain and immediately plunge into a bowl of ice water to stop the cooking. Once the peas have cooled, drain, pat dry, cut in half, and set aside.

4. Stand a mango on the stem end. Using a sharp knife, cut the mango into two large pieces, cutting as close to the large flat pit as possible. Score each half of the mango into 1-inch squares, but don't cut through the skin. Next, run the knife between the flesh and the skin to release the cubes. Place the cubes in a small bowl; repeat with the other mango. Squeeze excess juice from the trimmings into the bowl. Squeeze the lime onto the mango cubes and season with a little salt.

5. When the spaghetti is done, drain, rinse with cold water, and drain again. In a large bowl, toss the spaghetti with the peanut dressing until well coated. Add the peas and three quarters of the scallions and toss to combine. Place the noodles on a large serving platter, sprinkle the mango over the noodles, and garnish with the remaining scallions, the cilantro, and peanuts. Serve immediately. If making in advance, reserve about one third of the dressing and toss the noodles with the reserved dressing immediately before serving.

Rigatoni with Squash and Caramelized Onions

spungen
on prepeeled
squash
To save some prep
time, buy peeled
and cubed butternut
squash from the
supermarket. Make
sure it looks fresh
and not dry on the
outside; it won't have
as much flavor if it's
been sitting around.

All of my favorite fall flavors are combined in this incredibly rich and totally-worth-the-time-it-takes-to-prepare pasta dish (though it can be done up to a day ahead of time). It's absolutely perfect for a casual weekend buffet. Serve it with a big, crisp salad of spicy greens, and it's all you need.

SERVES 8 TO 10

Kosher salt

1 pound small rigatoni

1 large or 2 small butternut squash (about 4 pounds total)

2 ¼-inch-thick slices pancetta (about 4 ounces total), cubed

3 garlic cloves, thinly sliced

1 tablespoon unsalted butter

2 large onions, cut in half lengthwise and thickly sliced

Freshly ground black pepper

1 tablespoon olive oil

2 tablespoons rosemary leaves, finely chopped

1½ cups Golden Chicken Stock (page 207) or vegetable stock

1½ cups heavy cream

About 1½ cups freshly grated Parmigiano-Reggiano

½ pound Italian fontina, cut into ½-inch pieces

1. Bring a large pot of water to a boil. Add 1 teaspoon salt and the pasta to the water. Cook the pasta according to package directions, stirring occasionally, until just short of al dente; the pasta should still be white at the center when cut in half. (It will continue to cook in the oven.) Drain and rinse the pasta; set aside.

2. While the water is coming to a boil, cut the squash in half crosswise, separating the neck from the ball. Peel and seed both halves of the squash. Cut into ¾-inch chunks and set aside. Cook the pancetta in a 12-inch sauté pan (preferably nonstick) over medium-high heat, stirring frequently, until crisp and brown, about 10 minutes. Remove with a slotted spoon, transfer to a plate, and set aside.

3. Leaving 2 tablespoons of fat in the pan, add the garlic and sauté until golden brown, stirring frequently, about 5 minutes. Add the butter and onions and cook until golden brown, stirring occasionally, about 10 minutes. Reduce the heat to low, season with salt and pepper. Add ¼ cup water, cover, and cook for 5 more minutes. Remove the onions from the pan to a large bowl and set aside.

4. Add the oil, squash, half of the chopped rosemary, ½ teaspoon salt, and ¼ teaspoon pepper to the sauté pan and cook over high heat, stirring frequently, until tender when pierced with a paring knife, about 10 minutes. Add the stock and bring to a boil; reduce to a simmer and cook over medium heat. Cook until the squash has absorbed most of the liquid and is quite tender, 8 to 10 minutes, and the liquid that remains in the pan has thickened. If the squash is not tender, add some additional water and continue to simmer until tender. Add the cream and bring to a boil. Boil for 1 minute; remove from the heat.

5. Transfer the squash to a large bowl and cool slightly, stirring occasionally. Add the pasta, half of the onions, the pancetta, 1 cup of the Parmigiano, the fontina, and the remainder of the rosemary. Season with salt and pepper to taste. Stir gently to combine thoroughly. Transfer to a 4-quart baking dish and spread the remaining onions over the top. If baking right away, proceed to step 6. Otherwise, cover tightly with plastic wrap and refrigerate until ready to bake. The pasta can be made to this point up to one day in advance.

6. Preheat the oven to 350°F. Sprinkle about ½ cup Parmigiano over the top and transfer to the oven. Bake for about 45 minutes, until the top is golden brown and the sauce is bubbling. Serve immediately.

Golden Chicken Stock

If I go to the trouble of making homemade stock—and I do because it is well worth the effort—I want to get some poached chicken for salads and sandwiches out of the deal. That's why I always start with a whole chicken rather than necks and backs, as some people do. Use the cooked chicken meat in chicken salad for lunch, or add it to a pan of sautéed vegetables to go over pasta or rice for a quick dinner.

MAKES ABOUT 4 QUARTS

- 1 whole chicken (about 3½ pounds)
- 2 medium onions, unpeeled and halved
- 1 or 2 leeks, white part only, optional
- 2 celery stalks, cut into thirds

Small handful of celery leaves

- 2 or 3 parsnips, optional
- 3 small or 2 large carrots, scrubbed and cut into 4-inch pieces
- 2 mushrooms, or leftover mushroom stems, optional

Handful of flat-leaf parsley stems

A few thyme sprigs

- 1 scant teaspoon black peppercorns
- 1 bay leaf
- 1 teaspoon kosher salt, plus more to season chicken

1. Wash the chicken and place in a large stockpot. Add all remaining ingredients and fill with enough cold water to cover by 2 inches. Bring to a boil over high heat then reduce to a bare simmer. Simmer for 1 hour, skimming off the foam that rises to the top.

2. Remove the chicken by placing a large spoon in the cavity and carefully lifting it up. Drain any liquid over the pot before transferring the chicken to a plate. Let the chicken cool slightly, then carve off all white and dark meat, holding the chicken in place with a fork. Salt the chicken meat, cool slightly, cover, and refrigerate. Return the carcass and bones, along with any juices that accumulated on the plate, to the stockpot. Continue to simmer the stock for at least 1 hour more.

3. Strain the stock through a colander into a large bowl, and discard the solids. Strain again through a fine mesh sieve (lined with cheesecloth or a coffee filter if you have it) into another large bowl. Divide into small containers and let cool, then refrigerate until cold. Remove and discard the fat from the top, and freeze if not using right away. (If using immediately, skim off the fat using a wide flat spoon or use a fat separator.) Refrigerate for up to 4 days or freeze for up to 6 months.

TO MAKE A CLEAR, GOLDEN-HUED STOCK, FOLLOW THESE SIMPLE GUIDELINES: Use as many yellow onion skins as you have around, and don't bother peeling the ones for the stock. Their natural color will help tint the stock.

Avoid anything that's dark green, like parsley leaves (stems are okay) and the dark green tops of leeks. These will contribute to turning the stock a murky color.

Stock should be simmered over the lowest possible flame; you may not even see a bubble, only steam.

Resist the urge to stir the stock and break up the bones; the less you touch it, the clearer it will be.

Roasted Tomato Tart

SERVES 6 TO 8

¾ cup ricotta

¼ cup freshly grated Parmigiano-Reggiano, plus more for rolling
dough and sprinkling

½ teaspoon kosher salt

Freshly ground black pepper

2 large egg yolks

Handful of chopped fresh herbs such as oregano, thyme, or chives

½ recipe Tart Dough, prepared through step 2 and chilled (page 211)

10 to 15 Slow-Roasted Tomatoes (page 213)

2 teaspoons heavy cream or milk

1. Combine the ricotta, ¼ cup Parmigiano, salt, pepper, 1 egg yolk, and the
herbs in a small bowl. Stir until well combined. Set aside.

2. Dust a work surface with grated Parmigiano. Sprinkle more cheese on top of
the dough. Roll into a rough circle about 10 inches in diameter and ⅛ inch thick.
Turn frequently and dust with more cheese as needed to prevent sticking.
Transfer to a baking sheet lined with parchment.

3. Spread the filling on the dough, leaving about a 1½-inch border. Arrange the
tomatoes on top, leaving a little space between them, and gently fold the edges
of the dough toward the center, creating a 1- to 1½-inch border. Chill until firm.

4. Preheat the oven to 425°F, and position the rack in the middle of the oven.

5. Gently but firmly press the sides of the tart down with slightly cupped hands.
This will prevent the tart from unfurling while baking. In a small bowl, whisk
together the remaining egg yolk and the heavy cream. Brush the edges of the
tart with the egg wash and then sprinkle with grated Parmigiano. Immediately
transfer to the oven.

6. After 10 minutes, reduce the oven temperature to 400°F, rotate the baking
pan, and bake 20 minutes longer. The edges and bottom should be golden
brown. Remove from the oven and slide the tart, on the parchment paper, onto
a cooling rack. Serve warm or at room temperature.

editor's note

Spungen says that you
can slow-roast any size
or type of tomato but
notes that the timing
will vary depending
on the size. Shriveled
edges and just a bit of
wetness in the center
will indicate that the
tomatoes are done.

Roasted Tomato Tart

Tart Dough

MAKES TWO 8-INCH TART SHELLS

 2 cups all-purpose flour

½ teaspoon kosher salt

 1 teaspoon sugar

1½ sticks (12 tablespoons) cold unsalted butter, cut into ¼-inch pieces

Ice water

BASIC ROLLED DOUGH

1. Combine the flour, salt, and sugar in a chilled bowl and whisk to combine. Cut the cold butter into the flour using a pastry blender until the largest butter pieces are about the size of almonds. Using your hands, break down the biggest pieces of butter, rubbing them into the flour between your thumbs and fingers until the largest pieces are the size of large peas. Use a fork to stir as you dribble in 2 tablespoons to ¼ cup ice water, a little at a time. To test whether you've added enough water, squeeze a bit of the mixture in your hand to see if it holds together. Firmly press down on the dough in the bowl, giving it one or two kneads until it holds together in a mass.

2. Divide the dough in half. Place each half onto a piece of plastic wrap, loosely gather up the wrap, and firmly press down into a rough circle about 1 inch thick. Each disk of dough will be just the right size for one 8- to 10-inch tart. Chill until firm, at least 1 hour or overnight. The dough can also be frozen at this point for a month or two. Slip into a resealable plastic bag for freezing.

3. When you need to roll it out, let the dough soften until it is malleable, giving it a few whacks with a rolling pin to help it along. Lightly flour your work surface (see below) and roll the dough from the center out, using firm pressure, until it is about ⅛ inch thick, flipping it over and adding more flour to the work surface and top of dough as needed. Starting from the top edge of the dough, roll the dough onto the rolling pin, and then center and unroll it over the top of a tart pan with a removable bottom.

editor's note

For a simple, speedy variation on this crust, press the dough right into a tart pan and then chill completely. Spungen notes that this produces a perfectly good, if not quite as tender, crust.

spungen on serving the tart

I would serve this at lunch with a salad or as part of a buffet. It could also be served in thin slices as hors d'oeuvres. You can make this any shape you like because it's free-form, so you could do a long rectangle and slice it up and serve it as an appetizer.

4. Using your knuckles, nudge the dough down into the corners of the tart pan, being careful not to stretch it. Fold it gently over the edges of the pan, and run the rolling pin across the top to trim the edges. The edges of the pan will cut through the dough. Again, use your knuckles to gently press the dough against the side of the pan. Wrap in plastic wrap or slip into a resealable plastic bag and chill until ready to use. At this point, it can be refrigerated for 1 to 2 days, or frozen for a week or two.

5. To blind bake the shell, preheat the oven to 400°F. Prick the chilled tart shell all over with a fork. Line the tart with parchment paper or aluminum foil and fill with uncooked rice, beans, pie weights, or another tart pan of the same size to prevent the shell from rising. Fold the foil in toward the center to expose the edges of the pastry. Bake until the edges are golden brown, about 25 minutes. Remove the parchment paper and weights, and bake for an additional 5 to 10 minutes, until the bottom turns golden brown.

PRESS-IN METHOD

Prepare the Basic Rolled Dough through step 1. Divide the dough in half and place one half in a tart pan with a removable bottom. (Wrap the other half and refrigerate or freeze it for later use. Return to room temperature before using.) Working quickly so you don't warm the dough too much, spread it out evenly in the pan and up the sides, pressing with the flat side of your knuckles. Make sure the sides of the tart shell are about as thick as the bottom. Chill until very firm, at least 1 hour. Then proceed with your recipe.

FLAKY DOUGH

1. Combine the flour, salt, and sugar in a chilled bowl and whisk until combined. Cut the cold butter into the flour using a pastry blender until the butter pieces are between ¼ inch and ½ inch. Rub the largest butter pieces between your thumbs and fingers to break them down a bit more.

2. Use a fork to stir as you dribble in about ¼ cup ice water, a tablespoon at a time. To test whether you've added enough water, squeeze a bit in your hand to see if it holds together. If the dough seems dry, add another tablespoon or two of water and stir with the fork until the water is evenly distributed and absorbed.

Firmly press down on the dough in the bowl, giving it one or two kneads until it holds together in a rough mass. It will be quite raggedy.

3. Shape the dough into a long rectangle on a piece of plastic wrap. Fold the dough into thirds using the plastic wrap to help lift the dough. Cut into 2 equal pieces, wrap in plastic, and firmly press down on the plastic to compress the dough slightly. Refrigerate until firm, at least 1 hour or overnight. The dough can also be wrapped in plastic and frozen at this point for a month or two. To roll out the dough, follow step 3 for Basic Rolled Dough (page 211).

Slow-Roasted Tomatoes

MAKES ABOUT 24 PIECES

- 1 garlic clove
- 12 plum tomatoes
- About 2 tablespoons extra virgin olive oil
- 2 or 3 thyme sprigs
- 2 or 3 oregano sprigs
- Coarse sea salt

1. Preheat the oven to 350°F, and position the rack in the middle of the oven. Line 1 large or 2 smaller baking sheets with parchment paper.

2. Sliver the garlic as thinly as possible. Cut the tomatoes in half. Cut larger ones in quarters. Arrange the tomatoes, cut side up, on the baking sheet, leaving plenty of space in between. Drizzle each tomato with oil and rub with your fingers to coat well. Sprinkle with the garlic, herbs, and salt.

3. Reduce the oven to 300°F and bake for 2 to 2½ hours, until the tomatoes are shriveled and beginning to brown. Let cool, and transfer to an airtight container or jar if not using right away.

editor's note
Spungen likes to prep her work counter by wiping it with a moist paper towel, leaving the surface damp but not wet, so a light coating of flour will stick.

Caramel Apple Tart

SERVES 6 TO 8

1 cup sugar

3 tablespoons unsalted butter, cut into pieces

4 Granny Smith apples, peeled, cored, and each cut into 8 wedges

½ vanilla bean, or 1 teaspoon pure vanilla extract

Flour, for rolling

½ recipe Tart Dough (page 211)

1 large egg yolk

1 tablespoon heavy cream or milk

Homemade Crème Fraîche (page 216)

1. Make the caramelized apples: Stir together ⅔ cup water and the sugar in a large, heavy, light-colored frying or sauté pan no smaller than 10 inches. After this point, do not stir: just swirl the pan gently to keep the caramel cooking evenly. If you notice undissolved sugar on the sides of the pan, brush them down with water to prevent crystallization.

2. Cook over medium-high heat, swirling occasionally. As the caramel begins to darken, swirl more frequently to even out the color. Cook until the sugar is a dark amber color, 15 to 20 minutes, depending on the size and weight of the pan. If the sugar is cooking too quickly, reduce the heat to medium.

3. As soon as the caramel is ready, add the butter, immediately followed by the apples. The caramel will sputter a bit when the apples are added, so do so carefully. Toss well to combine.

4. Scrape the seeds from the vanilla bean half into the apple mixture and add the pod. Stir well to combine. Continue cooking over medium-high heat until the apples begin to turn transparent around the edges, about 15 minutes. After the initial stir, it is important that you gently toss the apples, rather than stir, so the apples do not fall apart. When the apples are done, turn off the heat. Add the vanilla extract, if using, and toss a few times. Immediately transfer the apples to a nonstick baking sheet. Using a wooden spoon, gently spread them into a single layer and let cool.

5. Line a baking sheet with parchment paper. On a lightly floured surface, roll the dough, working from the center out, into roughly a 14- × 16-inch rectangle. The dough should be no more than ¼ inch thick. Every few rolls, release the dough by running an offset spatula underneath, and sprinkle more flour under it. Drape the dough over a rolling pin and transfer to the baking sheet.

6. Arrange the apples in the center of the dough leaving a 1½-inch border. (If the caramel has hardened you can loosen it by placing the baking sheet in the oven for a few minutes.) Gently fold the edge of the crust up and over the apples, tearing off any excess dough if it's covering too much of the filling. There should be approximately a 2-inch edge of dough on all sides, with the center open. Refrigerate or freeze until firm.

7. While the tart is chilling, preheat the oven to 375°F and position a rack in the middle of the oven.

8. Whisk together the egg yolk and cream, and brush lightly on the edge of the tart. Bake the tart, rotating the pan halfway through, until the crust is golden and the apples are bubbling, about 35 minutes. Transfer to a wire rack and cool slightly. Serve warm or at room temperature with Homemade Crème Fraîche (recipe follows).

Homemade Crème Fraîche

MAKES 2 CUPS

  2 **cups heavy cream**
  2 **tablespoons buttermilk**

1. Combine the cream and buttermilk in a clean glass jar. Place the uncovered jar in a saucepan of barely simmering water. When the cream is just warm, remove it and cover tightly with plastic wrap or wax paper, using a rubber band to secure the wrap. Put the jar in a warm place, avoiding drafts.

2. Once thickened, after 12 to 24 hours, stir once, re-cover, and place in the refrigerator, where it will thicken even further and keep for about 2 weeks.

BEST OF THE BEST EXCLUSIVE

Tandoori Chicken Salad with Peach Raita

4 SERVINGS

1½ cups plain yogurt

1 small onion, minced

1 tablespoon plus 1 teaspoon fresh lime juice

¾ teaspoon cinnamon

1 teaspoon sweet paprika

1 teaspoon ground coriander

1 teaspoon ground cumin

2 large garlic cloves

2 medium jalapeños, seeded and minced

Kosher salt

4 skinless, boneless chicken breasts (about 1¾ pounds)

1 firm peach, cut into ½-inch dice

1 small Kirby cucumber, cut into ½-inch dice

Freshly ground pepper

1 bunch watercress

1 tablespoon extra-virgin olive oil

1. In a food processor, combine ¾ cup of the yogurt with all but 2 tablespoons of the onion. Add 1 tablespoon of the lime juice, the cinnamon, paprika, coriander, cumin, garlic, half of the jalapeños and 1 teaspoon of salt. Puree the marinade and transfer to a large baking dish. Add the chicken, cover and refrigerate for 4 hours.

2. To make the raita, combine the remaining yogurt, onion, lime juice and jalapeños in a bowl. Add the peach and cucumber. Cover and refrigerate.

3. Light a grill. Remove the chicken from the marinade and season with salt. Grill over moderately high heat for 6 minutes per side, or until cooked through.

4. Season the raita with salt and pepper. In a medium bowl, toss the watercress with the olive oil, salt and pepper. Slice the chicken breasts and serve with the raita and watercress salad.

editor's note

The yogurt marinade not only flavors the boneless chicken breast but also tenderizes it and keeps it moist. Make sure not to marinate the chicken for too long (over 6 hours) or the meat will get mushy.

One of many delightful Mariko Jesse
illustrations from *Sweet Gratitude.*

Sweet Gratitude

by Judith Sutton

In *Sweet Gratitude,* Judith Sutton's third book, she encourages readers to follow her example and bake a "thank you" for a hardworking teacher, helpful neighbor or friend in need, instead of just buying something from the store. This understated, sweetly old-fashioned book offers 70 phenomenally reliable, appealing recipes along with whimsical, charming illustrations. Once you bake a tray of her Amazing Toffee Thins or make her surprisingly simple Peanut Butter Pie with a Chocolate Cookie Crust, you'll be grateful for her excellent guidance.

Published by Artisan, 128 pages, $15.95.

BEST RECIPES

Amazing Toffee Thins
220

Ginger-Peach
Upside-Down Cake
221

Peanut Butter Pie with a
Chocolate Cookie Crust
223

Lemon Mousse
225

**BEST OF THE BEST
EXCLUSIVE**

Cherry–Brown Butter Tart
226

Find more recipes by
Judith Sutton at
foodandwine.com/sutton

Amazing Toffee Thins

MAKES 64 COOKIES

1¼ cups unbleached all-purpose flour

¼ teaspoon salt

12 tablespoons (1½ sticks) unsalted butter, at room temperature

¾ cup packed dark brown sugar

1½ teaspoons pure vanilla extract

1. Whisk together the flour and salt in a medium bowl.

2. In a large bowl, beat the butter and brown sugar with an electric mixer on medium speed until light and fluffy, 2 to 3 minutes. Scrape down the sides of the bowl. Beat in the vanilla. On low speed, beat in the flour in two additions.

3. Divide the dough in half and put each half on a square of waxed paper. Form each piece into a rough log, wrap loosely in the waxed paper, and refrigerate until firm enough to shape, about 45 minutes.

4. Roll each log of dough under the palms of your hands into an 8-inch-long cylinder (if the dough becomes sticky, refrigerate it briefly), then roll it up tightly in the waxed paper, using the paper to help make a smooth, compact log. Refrigerate until firm, 1½ to 2 hours. (The dough can be frozen, well wrapped, for up to 1 month. Thaw in the refrigerator before using.)

5. Put the racks in the upper and lower thirds of the oven and preheat the oven to 350°F.

6. Work with one log of dough at a time, keeping the second one refrigerated. Using a sharp heavy knife, cut the dough into ¼-inch-thick slices and place them about 2 inches apart on ungreased heavy baking sheets (if you don't have heavy baking sheets, reduce the baking time by a minute or two).

7. Bake for 10 to 12 minutes, rotating the baking sheets halfway through baking, until the cookies are golden brown around the edges. Let cool on the baking sheets for 3 minutes, then transfer the cookies to racks to cool completely. (The cookies can be stored in an airtight container for up to 3 days.)

Ginger-Peach Upside-Down Cake

SERVES 8

GINGER-PEACH TOPPING

- 4 tablespoons unsalted butter, cut into 4 pieces
- ¼ cup packed light brown sugar
- 2 cups canned peach slices in heavy syrup, thoroughly drained
- 2 tablespoons minced crystallized ginger

UPSIDE-DOWN CAKE

- 1⅓ cups unbleached all-purpose flour
- 1½ teaspoons baking powder
- ¼ teaspoon salt
- ½ teaspoon ground ginger
- 8 tablespoons (1 stick) unsalted butter, at room temperature
- 1 cup granulated sugar
- 2 large eggs
- 1½ teaspoons pure vanilla extract
- ½ cup whole milk

1. Put a rack in the middle of the oven and preheat the oven to 350°F.

FOR THE TOPPING

2. Melt the butter in a 9-inch round cake pan over low heat. Using a wooden spoon, stir in the brown sugar and cook, stirring, for about 3 minutes, or until the mixture is smooth and bubbling (it may look slightly grainy). Remove the pan from the heat.

3. Lay the peach slices on a double layer of paper towels and gently blot away excess moisture with another paper towel. Reserve 5 or 6 of the smaller slices for the center of the cake. Arrange the remaining slices side by side, without crowding, in a ring on the brown sugar mixture, about ¼ inch from the sides of the pan. Arrange the reserved slices in a pinwheel pattern in the center. Sprinkle the crystallized ginger evenly over the peaches. Set aside.

sutton on canned peaches

I know it may seem odd to choose canned fruit over fresh in this recipe, but it actually works better. Sometimes fresh peaches just aren't juicy enough, whereas the canned ones are always ripe.

blueberry-lemon cake variation

For a blueberry-lemon upside-down cake, increase the brown sugar in the topping to ⅔ cup. Substitute 2 cups fresh blueberries, rinsed and thoroughly drained, for the peaches. Omit the crystallized ginger and sprinkle 1½ teaspoons grated lemon zest over the blueberries in the pan. For the batter, omit the ground ginger and add 1½ teaspoons grated lemon zest along with the vanilla. Bake as directed.

FOR THE CAKE

4. Whisk together the flour, baking powder, salt, and ground ginger in a small bowl.

5. In a large bowl, beat the butter and granulated sugar with an electric mixer on medium speed until light and fluffy, 2 to 3 minutes. Scrape down the sides of the bowl. Add the eggs one at a time, beating well after each addition. Beat in the vanilla. On low speed, beat in half the flour, then beat in the milk. Beat in the remaining flour just until incorporated.

6. Spoon the batter in large dollops over the peaches. Using a rubber spatula, carefully spread the batter over the peaches without disturbing them, covering them completely and making sure the batter reaches the edges of the pan (the peaches will be juicy).

7. Bake for 40 to 45 minutes, or until a toothpick inserted in the center of the cake comes out clean. Cool the cake in the pan on a wire rack for 3 minutes.

8. Run a knife around the edge of the pan to release the cake. Invert a wire rack over the cake, then invert the cake onto the rack and lift off the pan. (If any peach slices have stuck to the pan, replace them on top of the cake.) Set the rack on a baking sheet to catch any juices. Serve warm or at room temperature. The cooled cake can be stored, covered, at room temperature for up to 1 day.

Peanut Butter Pie with a Chocolate Cookie Crust

Peanut butter pie is a guilty pleasure that is impossible to resist. The classic filling for this all-American dessert includes cream cheese, which adds to its richness; it also gives the filling a slight tang, which some people love, but some—as I learned—don't. So I also make a somewhat lighter (though no less rich) variation without cream cheese, and I've included both versions here. Either one takes only minutes to put together, but the filling and chocolate topping do need time to chill. In fact, the filling tastes more peanut buttery if you refrigerate it overnight.

SERVES 10

CHOCOLATE COOKIE CRUST

1½ cups chocolate wafer cookie crumbs (from about 25 cookies, such as Nabisco Famous Wafers)

 5 tablespoons unsalted butter, melted

PEANUT BUTTER FILLING

 1 cup smooth peanut butter (not "natural style")

 6 ounces cream cheese, cut into chunks

 1 cup confectioners' sugar

 1 cup heavy cream

1½ teaspoons pure vanilla extract

CHOCOLATE GANACHE TOPPING

 5 ounces bittersweet or semisweet chocolate, coarsely chopped

½ cup heavy cream

FOR THE CRUST

1. Combine the cookie crumbs and melted butter in a medium bowl, stirring until the crumbs are evenly moistened. Press the mixture firmly and evenly over the bottom and up the sides of a 9-inch pie pan (use a flat-bottomed drinking glass to press the crumbs over the bottom of the pan). Refrigerate for 30 minutes to set the crust.

FOR THE FILLING

2. In a large bowl, beat the peanut butter, cream cheese, and confectioners' sugar with an electric mixer on medium speed until smooth and creamy.

3. In a bowl, beat (no need to wash the beaters) the cream and vanilla until the cream holds soft peaks. Using a rubber spatula, stir ½ cup of the whipped cream into the peanut butter mixture to lighten it, then fold in the remaining cream in two batches. Scrape the filling into the chilled piecrust, mounding it slightly in the center. Refrigerate for at least 1 hour, or until the filling is cold.

FOR THE TOPPING

4. Put the chocolate in a food processor and process until finely chopped. Bring the cream to a boil in a small saucepan. With the machine on, pour in the hot cream and process just until the chocolate is completely melted, stopping to scrape down the sides of the bowl once or twice. Pour the chocolate mixture into a 2-cup glass measure or a small bowl with a pour spout and let cool to room temperature (the topping should still be fluid enough to pour).

5. Pour the topping evenly over the top of the chilled pie, spreading it evenly with a long metal spatula. Refrigerate the pie for at least 4 hours. (The pie can be refrigerated for up to 1 day.)

6. Use a hot knife (dipped into hot water and wiped dry between each slice) to cut the pie into wedges.

WHIPPED CREAM PEANUT BUTTER PIE

Prepare and chill the crust as directed. For the filling, use ¾ cup peanut butter, ¾ cup confectioners' sugar, 1½ cups heavy cream, and 1 teaspoon pure vanilla extract; omit the cream cheese. In a bowl, combine the peanut butter and ¼ cup of the confectioners' sugar and beat well. In another bowl, combine the cream, the remaining ½ cup confectioners' sugar, and the vanilla and beat (no need to wash the beaters) until firm peaks form. Stir ½ cup of the whipped cream into the peanut butter, then gently but thoroughly fold in the remaining cream; do not overmix. Scrape the filling into the pie shell and refrigerate for at least 2 hours. Just before serving, garnish with chocolate curls or shavings.

Lemon Mousse

SERVES 6 TO 8

   6 tablespoons unsalted butter, cut into chunks
   4 large egg yolks
   ¾ cup sugar
1½ tablespoons grated lemon zest
   ¾ cup fresh lemon juice (from 4 large lemons)
   2 to 3 cups heavy cream
   3 to 4½ tablespoons sugar

1. Melt the butter in a large saucepan (preferably not aluminum, which could react with the lemon juice) over medium heat. Remove the pan from the heat and set it aside.

2. In a medium bowl, beat the egg yolks and ¾ cup sugar with an electric mixer on medium speed until thick and pale, about 2 minutes. On low speed, beat in the lemon zest and juice until thoroughly blended. Transfer the mixture to the saucepan of butter and cook over low to medium-low heat, stirring constantly with a wooden spoon or a heatproof spatula, until the filling is very thick and coats the back of the spoon, 7 to 10 minutes; do not let the custard boil.

3. Strain the custard through a sieve (to remove the lemon zest) into a small bowl and let cool. Cover and refrigerate it until cold, at least 2 hours. (The custard can be made up to 5 days ahead.)

4. Combine the cream and sugar (use 1½ tablespoons sugar for each cup of cream) in a large bowl and beat until the cream just holds firm peaks. Using a rubber spatula, gently but thoroughly fold the custard into the cream.

5. Transfer the mousse to a serving bowl or individual serving dishes and refrigerate for at least 1 hour. (The mousse can be refrigerated, tightly covered, for up to 1 day.)

editor's note

Sutton says that this recipe is easy to adapt by varying the amount of cream. Use 3 cups for a creamier version or 2 to 2½ cups for a more lemony and slightly denser version. The custard base keeps extremely well, so you can make it up to five days ahead.

Cherry–Brown Butter Tart

editor's note
Browning the butter
in this pie filling
gives it a rich, nutty
flavor. Watch the
butter carefully as
it turns from yellow
to brown, since it
can quickly become
burnt and bitter.

8 SERVINGS

PASTRY

1¼ cups all-purpose flour

¼ cup confectioners' sugar

Salt

6 tablespoons cold unsalted butter, cut into ½-inch pieces

3 tablespoons ice water

FILLING

1 stick plus 3 tablespoons unsalted butter

1 vanilla bean, split, seeds scraped

3 large eggs

1 cup granulated sugar

Salt

¼ cup all-purpose flour

½ pound fresh cherries, pitted and halved, or one 10-ounce bag frozen cherries, thawed and drained

Confectioners' sugar, for dusting

1. Make the Pastry: In a food processor, pulse the flour with the sugar and a pinch of salt. Add the butter and pulse several times, until it is the size of small peas. Pour in the ice water and pulse just until the crumbs are evenly moistened. Turn the pastry out onto a work surface and gather it into a ball. Flatten into a disk, wrap in plastic and refrigerate for at least 30 minutes.

2. Preheat the oven to 375°. On a lightly floured surface, roll out the pastry to a 12-inch round. Ease the pastry into a 9-inch fluted tart pan with a removable bottom and trim the edges. Refrigerate for 30 minutes, until firm.

3. Line the pastry with foil and fill it with pie weights or dried beans. Bake in the lower third of the oven for 20 minutes, until the pastry is set. Remove the foil and pie weights and bake for 10 minutes longer, until the shell is light golden and just cooked through. Transfer the tart shell to a rack to cool. Reduce the oven temperature to 350°.

4. Make the Filling: In a small saucepan, cook the butter with the vanilla bean and seeds over moderately high heat until it turns a deep golden brown, about 6 minutes. Discard the vanilla bean. Let the butter cool slightly.

5. In a medium bowl, whisk the eggs with the granulated sugar and a pinch of salt until blended. Whisk in the flour, then gradually whisk in the brown butter until fully incorporated.

6. Spread the cherries in the tart shell in an even layer. Pour the brown butter filling over the cherries and bake in the center of the oven for 35 minutes, or until the top of the tart is golden brown and the filling is set. Transfer the tart to a rack to cool completely. Just before serving, generously dust the cooled tart with confectioners' sugar.

MAKE AHEAD The tart can be made up to 6 hours ahead.

Minted Lentil and Goat
Cheese Strudel, p. 230

The Herbal Kitchen

by Jerry Traunfeld

"When I cook on my nights off, I don't want to feel like I'm at work—I just cook food that I crave," says Jerry Traunfeld, the stellar chef at The Herbfarm Restaurant near Seattle. "And when I cook with fresh herbs, it's easy to achieve amazing results with little effort." Traunfeld encourages readers to grow herbs as well as experiment with them in the kitchen, listing sources for seeds, plants and equipment.

Published by William Morrow, 272 pages, $34.95.

Find more recipes by
Jerry Traunfeld at
foodandwine.com/traunfeld

Minted Lentil and Goat Cheese Strudel

traunfeld on mint

There are many different kinds of mint. When you buy mint at the grocery store, there's never a label or sign that says what kind it is, but it's always spearmint. But if you get it at the farmers' market, you might want to ask what kind it is. Spearmint has a nice fruity quality; peppermint has a lot of menthol and is almost toothpastey. Spearmint is the one to use for savory food.

When you bite into this strudel, you'll find it hard to believe that it's made with lentils. Lentils combined with mint, thyme, and goat cheese becomes a richly flavored filling that almost tastes as if it were made with lamb.

Be sure to follow the phyllo's package directions for defrosting and handling; the dough is easy to work with when fresh and in good condition, but frustrating if the sheets become dry and torn. Phyllo sheets vary in size, depending on the brand, but the 9 x 14-inch size seems the most common; cut them to that size if they are larger. Once assembled, the strudels can be refrigerated until you are ready to bake them.

SIX 12-INCH STRUDELS; ABOUT 48 PIECES

 2 tablespoons olive oil
½ large onion, finely chopped
 1 clove garlic, finely chopped
 1 cup dry French-style lentils, such as *lentilles du Puy*
1¾ cups water
1½ teaspoons kosher salt
1½ tablespoons chopped thyme
¼ cup chopped spearmint
¼ cup chopped flat-leaf parsley
Freshly ground black pepper
 6 ounces soft goat cheese
24 sheets phyllo dough, 9 × 14 inches
12 tablespoons (6 ounces) unsalted butter, melted

Heat the olive oil in a small saucepan over medium heat and cook the onion and garlic in it until they soften, about 3 minutes. Stir in the lentils, water, and salt and bring to a boil. Lower the heat to a simmer, cover the pan, and cook until the lentils are tender, about 45 minutes. Transfer the lentils to a mixing bowl, draining off any liquid that might be left, and stir in the herbs and a good grinding of black pepper. Stir in the goat cheese.

Open up the package of phyllo. Always keep the sheets covered with a piece of plastic wrap and then a damp towel to keep them from drying out while you are working. Lift one sheet of phyllo and lay it on a piece of parchment paper. Brush the entire surface with melted butter. Cover with another piece of phyllo and more butter, and repeat until you have 4 layers with butter on the top. Divide the filling into 6 equal parts and form one part into a cylinder across the long side of the phyllo, about an inch from the edge. Lift the edge of the dough to begin to cover the filling, then grab the parchment from two corners and lift it so that the strudel rolls itself up loosely. It's important not to roll it tightly or the filling will burst through the side as it expands in the oven. Lift the strudel onto a baking sheet lined with parchment and brush it with more melted butter. Form the remaining 5 strudels in the same way.

Preheat the oven to 375°F. Bake the strudels for 25 to 30 minutes, or until golden brown. Expect a small amount of the filling to pop out of the open ends as it bakes. Let cool on the pan until warm, then transfer to a board, and cut each strudel into 8 pieces.

Tarragon Chicken Breasts with Buttered Leeks

traunfeld on substitutes
Instead of using tarragon, stir in 2 tablespoons chopped marjoram or ½ cup chopped dill or chervil.

4 SERVINGS

- 2 cups thinly sliced leeks, white and light green parts only (1 large or 2 small)
- 2 cups chicken broth
- 4 tablespoons unsalted butter
- 4 boneless skinless chicken breasts, about 1½ pounds
- Kosher salt and freshly ground black pepper
- 2 teaspoons fresh lemon juice
- 2 tablespoons coarsely chopped tarragon

Put the leeks in a large skillet with the chicken broth and 2 tablespoons of the butter. Cook them at a gentle boil over medium heat until they are tender and the broth has boiled down far enough that the leeks are no longer completely submerged. This should take about 8 minutes.

Sprinkle both sides of the chicken breasts with salt and pepper. Place them on top of the simmering leeks, spoon some of the leeks over the chicken, and cover the pan tightly.

Reduce the heat to low. In 10 minutes test the chicken for doneness. It should feel firm when you press on it, and if you cut a slit into the thickest part of a breast, there should be no sign of translucence. If the breast pieces are large, it could take as much as 15 minutes, but don't overcook them.

When the chicken is done, lift the pieces from the leeks and put them on a warm platter. Increase the heat under the leeks to high and stir in the lemon juice, the remaining 2 tablespoons butter, and the tarragon. When the butter melts, taste the sauce and add salt and pepper if you think it needs it. Pour the leek sauce over the chicken and serve.

Mushroom Marjoram Bread Pudding

10 SERVINGS

1	ounce dried porcini mushrooms

One (20- to 24-ounce) loaf rustic white bread, crust removed

6	tablespoons unsalted butter, softened
1	large onion, chopped
1	pound button or cremini mushrooms, rinsed and sliced
¼	cup chopped marjoram
6	large eggs
3	cups milk, whole or low fat
1	tablespoon kosher salt and ¼ teaspoon black pepper

Preheat the oven to 375°F. Put the dried mushrooms in a 2-cup liquid measuring cup and fill it with hot water. Dice the bread into rough 1-inch cubes. Smear the interior of a large shallow baking dish (at least 9 × 13 inches) with 2 tablespoons of the butter.

Lift the dried mushrooms out of their soaking liquid so that any grit they have released stays at the bottom of the cup. Chop them finely. Pour the mushroom soaking liquid through a fine strainer, agitating it as little as possible and keeping the last ½ cup or so of liquid behind.

Melt the remaining butter in a large skillet over medium heat and cook the onion in it until it softens, about 5 minutes. Add the sliced button mushrooms and the chopped porcini and cook them for another 5 minutes. Pour in the strained liquid and simmer for another 5 minutes. Stir in the marjoram and turn off the heat.

Whisk the eggs, milk, salt, and pepper together in a very large mixing bowl. Stir in the cooked mushrooms and onion. Add the bread cubes and gently toss them with a rubber spatula. Pour the pudding into the buttered baking dish. Bake for 50 to 55 minutes, or until browned on the top and firm to the touch in the center.

Shrimp in Garlic-Sage Butter

I've prepared shrimp a hundred ways, but I never enjoy them as much as when they're cooked unpeeled in a skillet with lots of butter and garlic. The only way I've found to improve on that is to add a handful of fresh sage leaves. Grab a stack of paper napkins, a loaf of crusty bread, a crisp white wine, and dig in.

2 SERVINGS

1 **pound very large shrimp (10 to 16)**

8 **tablespoons (4 ounces) unsalted butter, cut into cubes**

4 **cloves garlic, finely chopped**

Leaves from a 1-ounce bunch sage (16 to 20)

Coarse sea salt

Holding a shrimp with the legs pointing down, stick the tip of the bottom blade of a pair of scissors into the head end. Cut along the backside, slicing about a quarter of the way down into the flesh. Repeat with the rest of the shrimp. Rinse them under running water, removing the dark vein that runs along the backs. Pat them dry on paper towels.

Put the butter, garlic, and sage leaves in a large skillet over medium heat and stir from time to time. When the garlic begins to show the first signs of browning and the sage leaves are speckled with darker green spots, add the shrimp. Stir them around, lower the heat to medium-low, and cook uncovered for 5 to 8 minutes, turning them once, or until the shells are pink, the shrimp curl a bit, and the flesh no longer looks translucent. Spoon the shrimp into warm shallow bowls and pour any remaining butter and sage leaves over the top. Sprinkle with salt or offer it in small dishes at the table. Peel the shrimp as you eat them and soak up the butter with crusty bread.

Penne with Walnut Pesto and Eggplant

4 SERVINGS

2 small or 1 large eggplant (1½ pounds)
2 tablespoons olive oil
1 teaspoon kosher salt

PESTO
2 cups lightly packed basil leaves (2 ounces)
½ cup toasted walnuts
2 cloves garlic
½ teaspoon kosher salt
¼ cup olive oil
½ cup freshly grated Parmigiano-Reggiano

¾ pound penne pasta
½ cup roughly chopped toasted walnuts to finish

Preheat the oven to 425°F. Cut the unpeeled eggplant into ¾-inch cubes. Spread them out on a baking sheet that is either nonstick or lined with parchment paper. Drizzle with the olive oil and sprinkle with 1 teaspoon salt. Toss the cubes with your hands to distribute the oil and salt as evenly as you can and shake them out into a single layer. Bake the cubes for 25 to 30 minutes, or until they brown on the edges and are very soft.

While the eggplant is roasting, bring a large pot of salted water to a boil. Prepare the pesto by pulsing the basil, walnuts, garlic, and ½ teaspoon salt in a food processor. With the machine running, pour in the olive oil. Scrape down the bowl and add the cheese, then pulse again until combined.

Boil the pasta until it is tender but still slightly firm. Scoop ½ cup of the cooking water into a measuring cup, and drain the pasta. Return to the pot, top with the pesto, pour in the water, and stir until it is evenly sauced. Scrape the eggplant into the pot and stir gently. Scoop the pasta into a warmed large serving bowl or individual shallow bowls, sprinkle with the walnuts, and serve right away.

BEST OF THE BEST EXCLUSIVE

Fennel-Crusted Salmon Braised with Pinot Noir

4 SERVINGS

- 1 tablespoon fennel seeds
- 1 tablespoon coriander seeds
- ¼ teaspoon black peppercorns
- 1 teaspoon finely grated lemon zest

Kosher salt

Four 6-ounce skinless salmon fillets

- 3 tablespoons extra-virgin olive oil
- 2 medium leeks, white and light green parts only, halved lengthwise and thinly sliced crosswise
- 1 medium fennel bulb—halved lengthwise, cored and thinly sliced, fronds chopped and reserved (2 tablespoons)
- ½ cup dry red wine, such as Pinot Noir
- ½ cup chicken stock or low-sodium broth

1. In a spice grinder, combine the fennel seeds, coriander seeds, peppercorns, lemon zest and 2 teaspoons of kosher salt and grind to a powder. Reserve 1 tablespoon of the spice mixture. Season both sides of the salmon fillets with the remaining spice mixture.

2. In a large nonstick skillet, heat 2 tablespoons of the olive oil. Cook the salmon fillets over moderately high heat until lightly browned outside but still raw in the center, transfer to a plate and keep warm.

3. Add the remaining 1 tablespoon of olive oil to the skillet. Add the leeks, fennel, reserved 1 tablespoon of the spice mixture and a pinch of salt. Cook over moderate heat until the vegetables are just tender, about 5 minutes. Pour the wine and stock into the skillet and bring to a simmer. Set the salmon fillets on the vegetables, cover the skillet and cook over moderately low heat until the fish is just cooked through, about 8 minutes. Spoon the vegetables onto plates and top with the salmon fillets. Drizzle the sauce over the fish, sprinkle with the chopped fennel fronds and serve.

editor's note

This recipe combines two Northwestern regional specialties, Pinot Noir and salmon, in an unconventional way—seared fillets get cooked in a mixture of red wine and water.

Coca with Candied
Red Peppers, p. 240

The New Spanish Table

by Anya von Bremzen

Anya von Bremzen's latest book is well timed: Spain's avant-garde chefs have captured the world's attention with their brilliant ideas. But while Von Bremzen is passionate about these chefs, she stresses that Spanish cooking is firmly rooted in tradition: "The divide between high and low, haute and homey, classic and iconoclastic, rustic and refined can be deliciously blurred." She's as enthusiastic about old-fashioned dishes as she is about innovations like Catalan Guacamole and Creamy Basque Smoked Cheese Risotto.

Published by Workman, 496 pages, $35.

BEST RECIPES

Coca with Candied
Red Peppers
240

Catalan Guacamole
241

Creamy Basque Smoked
Cheese Risotto
242

Grilled Asparagus with
Honey and Sherry Vinegar
244

**BEST OF THE BEST
EXCLUSIVE**

Georgian Cheese Pie
245

Find more recipes by
Anya von Bremzen at
**foodandwine.com/
vonbremzen**

Coca with Candied Red Peppers

Coca con Pimientos Rojos Caramelizados

editor's note

Coca is a kind of Spanish-Mediterranean pizza topped with red peppers sweetened with confectioners' sugar. Von Bremzen describes it as a cross between a dessert tart and a savory pizza and says it's delicious with crisp, chilled rosé.

MAKES 1 LARGE COCA; SERVES 12 AS A TAPA

2 tablespoons olive oil, plus more for brushing the coca

1 medium-size white onion, quartered and thinly sliced

4 cups thinly sliced drained roasted peppers in oil (from four 14- to 16-ounce jars)

5 tablespoons granulated sugar

2 tablespoons sherry vinegar, preferably aged, or best-quality red wine vinegar

Coarse salt (kosher or sea)

All-purpose flour, for dusting the rolling pin

1 pound store-bought pizza dough, thawed if frozen

Confectioners' sugar, for dusting the coca

1. Heat the 2 tablespoons olive oil in a large skillet over medium-low heat. Add the onion and cook until limp but not browned, 5 to 7 minutes, stirring occasionally. Add the roasted peppers and cook for about 5 minutes, stirring. Add the granulated sugar, vinegar, and 2 tablespoons water and stir until the sugar dissolves. Cover the skillet, reduce the heat to low, and cook until the liquid is reduced, about 10 minutes, stirring from time to time. Season with salt to taste and let the pepper mixture cool completely.

2. Place an oven rack in the center of the oven and preheat the oven to 450°F. Lightly brush a 17-by-11-inch baking sheet with olive oil.

3. Lightly flour a work surface. Using a floured rolling pin, roll out the dough so it is roughly as large as the baking sheet. Transfer it to the oiled baking sheet and brush it with olive oil. Spread the filling evenly on top.

4. Bake the *coca* on the center rack until it is light golden and baked through, 18 to 20 minutes. Let the *coca* cool to warm (or make the *coca* ahead, which actually adds to its flavor; reheat it gently before serving). Cut the *coca* into rectangles (I use sturdy kitchen scissors for this), dust it very lightly with confectioners' sugar, and serve at once.

Catalan Guacamole

Guacamole a la Catalana

Barcelona might be as generously supplied with sushi joints as any other cosmopolitan city, but "fusion" cuisine of any kind is still regarded there with great suspicion. Witness the uproar that ensued when Juanito, the legendary proprietor of Bar Pinotxo in the Boqueria market, introduced a toasted canapé topped with avocado spread on his menu. How could a place as iconically Catalan as Pinotxo dare to spread a tostada with a Mexican guacamole, the traditionalists cried out. Could this be the end of Catalan cuisine? None of it seemed to bother Juanito, who proudly plied regulars with his new concoction. Besides, his lemony avocado spread, bolstered with sherry vinegar, isn't exactly guacamole. Juanito serves it on long slices of toasted bread, topped with fat anchovies and sprinkled with chopped, briny black olives.

MAKES ABOUT 1½ CUPS

- 2 small garlic cloves, chopped
- 2 best-quality oil-packed anchovy fillets, drained and chopped
- 3 tablespoons minced fresh flat-leaf parsley
- 1 large pinch of coarse salt (kosher or sea)
- 1½ tablespoons fragrant extra-virgin olive oil
- 1 tablespoon sherry vinegar, preferably aged
- 2 tablespoons fresh lemon juice, or more to taste
- 2 small ripe Hass avocados, pitted and diced
- 1 small ripe plum tomato, cut in half and grated on a box grater, skin discarded

Toasted or grilled country bread, for serving

1. Place the garlic, anchovies, parsley, and salt in a mortar and, using a pestle, mash them into a paste. Whisk in the olive oil, vinegar, and lemon juice. Set the dressing aside.

2. Place the avocados in a bowl and, using a fork, mash them until completely smooth. Stir in the tomato and the dressing, then taste for seasoning, adding more lemon juice as necessary. Let the spread stand for 15 to 20 minutes for the flavors to meld, then serve with toasted or grilled bread.

Creamy Basque Smoked Cheese Risotto
Arroz Cremoso con Idiazábal

Like the rest of the world, Spain has eagerly embraced Italian dishes, especially risotto, which is quite similar in texture to *caldoso*- or *meloso*-style soupy Spanish rice dishes. In the Basque Country, where tastes run to mild comfort food, a delicious risotto enriched with the local smoked Idiazábal cheese is one of the favorite restaurant staples. This recipe, from the Cuchara de San Telmo tapas bar in San Sebastián, is absolutely sensational—better than most of the risottos I have had in Italy. Sometimes, the chefs drizzle green herb oil and old balsamic vinegar on their tapas-scaled portions; on other occasions they add Catalan *allioli* for a garlicky kick. The dish is great as a first course or as a bed for seared scallops or other fish. If smoked Idiazábal cheese is not available, substitute another smoked cheese, such as Gouda or mozzarella.

SERVES 4 TO 6

1½ tablespoons olive oil

½ cup finely sliced scallions, including a bit of the green

2 large garlic cloves, minced

1½ cups best-quality risotto rice, preferably carnaroli

½ cup dry white wine

5½ to 6 cups chicken stock or broth, kept at a simmer

⅓ cup heavy (whipping) cream

1 cup shredded smoked cheese, such as Idiazábal or Gouda

⅓ cup freshly grated Parmesan cheese, preferably Parmigiano-Reggiano

2 to 3 tablespoons Parsley Oil (recipe follows)

3 tablespoons syrupy aged balsamic vinegar, or ⅓ cup thin balsamic vinegar reduced over medium-high heat to 3 tablespoons

1. Heat the olive oil in a heavy wide 3-quart saucepan, over medium-low heat. Add the scallions and cook, stirring, until soft but not browned, about 5 minutes. Add the garlic and stir for 30 seconds. Add the rice and stir for about 1 minute. Increase the heat to medium, add the wine, and stir vigorously until the wine is absorbed, 2 to 3 minutes.

2. Add 3 cups of the simmering stock, about 1 cup at a time, stirring constantly with a wooden spoon until each addition of liquid is absorbed. Continue adding the remaining stock, ½ cup at a time, stirring after each addition. Cook until the rice is tender but a little al dente, about 20 minutes total.

3. Add the cream, smoked cheese, and Parmesan and stir vigorously until the cheese melts, 1 to 2 minutes. Immediately spoon the risotto into serving bowls and drizzle some of the Parsley Oil and balsamic vinegar over each portion. Serve at once.

Parsley Oil
Aceite de Perejil

Parsley oil brightens the appearance and flavor of many dishes—gazpachos, risottos, grilled fish, or cream soups.

MAKES ABOUT ¼ CUP

⅓ cup extra-virgin olive oil
½ cup chopped fresh flat-leaf parsley

Place the olive oil and the parsley in a blender and puree until bright green and completely smooth. Let the oil stand at room temperature for at least 15 minutes or up to 2 hours, then strain it through a fine-mesh sieve into a bowl. The oil can be prepared up to several hours ahead.

Grilled Asparagus with Honey and Sherry Vinegar

Esparragos con Miel y Vinagre de Jerez

von bremzen on piquillo peppers

I'm completely obsessed with piquillo peppers—I love them. I put them on everything: I use them as a garnish, as a stuffing, simply sautéed. They're so sweet and so addictive.

This is one of those Spanish dishes that leaves you wondering how something so elemental—little more than asparagus, vinegar, and honey—can taste so memorable. It also makes you appreciate the transformational effects of good salt. Here I recommend a delicate flaky variety, such as Maldon, beloved by Spanish chefs. Make this in the spring when the asparagus is fat but tender. If you don't have a grill, asparagus is just as delicious broiled.

SERVES 4 TO 6

2 pounds beautiful fat asparagus, trimmed

4 tablespoons fragrant extra-virgin olive oil

1½ teaspoons honey

3 tablespoons sherry vinegar, preferably aged

Coarse salt (kosher or sea) and freshly ground black pepper

Flaky sea salt, such as Maldon, for serving

1. Light the grill and preheat it to medium or preheat the broiler.

2. Using a vegetable peeler, scrape off the tough outer skin from the lower stalks of the asparagus. Rinse the asparagus, pat it dry with paper towels, and toss with 1 tablespoon of the olive oil.

3. Place the honey, vinegar, and the remaining 3 tablespoons olive oil in a small bowl and whisk to mix. Season lightly with coarse salt and pepper and set aside.

4. Grill or broil the asparagus until tender and only lightly charred, turning once, about 3 minutes per side.

5. Arrange the asparagus on a serving plate, toss with the sauce, and sprinkle flaky sea salt on top. Serve at once.

The New
Spanish Table

ANYA VON BREMZEN

BEST OF THE BEST EXCLUSIVE

Georgian Cheese Pie

8 MAIN-COURSE AND 12 HORS D'OEUVRE SERVINGS

½ pound shredded mozzarella cheese

½ pound feta cheese, crumbled

⅓ cup chopped mixed fresh herbs, such as dill, cilantro and basil

1 large egg, beaten

¼ teaspoon freshly ground pepper

All-purpose flour, for dusting

One 17-ounce package puff pastry, thawed

1 large egg yolk beaten with 1 teaspoon milk, for brushing

1. Preheat the oven to 375°. Line a large baking sheet with foil. In a medium bowl, mix the mozzarella with the feta, herbs, whole egg and pepper.

2. On a lightly floured work surface, roll out 1 sheet of the puff pasty to a 10-by-15-inch rectangle and transfer it to the prepared baking sheet. Spread the cheese mixture evenly over the pastry, leaving a 1-inch border all around. Roll the second pastry sheet slightly larger than the first and set it over the cheese filling. Fold the edges of the bottom pastry up over the top and pinch to seal.

3. Brush the egg yolk mixture over the pastry. With a fork, prick a few holes in the top. Bake the pie for 30 minutes, or until golden brown. Let cool for at least 15 minutes before serving.

MAKE AHEAD The pie can be prepared through Step 2 and refrigerated overnight. The finished pie can be kept at room temperature for up to 3 hours.

editor's note

When Von Bremzen isn't testing recipes, she likes to cook dishes that remind her of growing up in Russia. Her mother developed this recipe as a quick variation on *khachapuri*, a classic cheese pie from the nearby Republic of Georgia.

Rib Chop Florentine, p. 248

The New American Steakhouse Cookbook

by David Walzog and Andrew Friedman

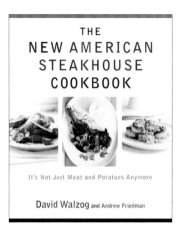

David Walzog, executive chef at The Country Club restaurant at Wynn Las Vegas hotel, has gained a reputation for modernizing the traditional American steak house menu. In his first cookbook, he provides excellent recipes for porterhouse and creamed spinach but goes far beyond. He steams littleneck clams in a bold roasted tomato broth and infuses oven-cooked beef short ribs with smoky, sweet barbecue flavors. The recipes are sometimes complex but reward the effort with distinctive, potent flavors.

Published by Broadway Books, 224 pages, $27.50.

BEST RECIPES

Rib Chop Florentine
248

Barbecue-Braised Beef Short Ribs
249

Chopped Vegetable Salad with Smoked Bacon and Red Wine Vinaigrette
250

Steamed Littleneck Clams, Roasted Tomato Broth, and Grilled Sourdough Bread
253

BEST OF THE BEST EXCLUSIVE

Crab and Avocado Salad with Creamy Herb Dressing
255

Find more recipes by David Walzog at
foodandwine.com/walzog

Rib Chop Florentine

A traditional Tuscan recipe, rib chop Florentine is served sliced with extra virgin olive oil, caramelized garlic, and fresh rosemary. This steak cut is a bit more difficult to cook due to the quantity of fat, both on the outside and running through the meat. This all but guarantees flare-ups, so don't leave the steak unattended on the grill; it can catch on fire and burn in a matter of seconds.

SERVES 2

½ cup extra virgin olive oil

4 garlic cloves, thinly sliced

4 fresh rosemary sprigs, roughly picked of some leaves (reserve a sprig with some leaves left on for garnish)

2-pound rib chop, 2 to 2¼ inches thick

Kosher salt

Freshly ground black pepper

Season and cook the rib chop until you achieve the desired char on the first side, approximately 10 minutes, moving it when necessary to avoid flare-ups. Turn it over and reduce the heat to medium if using a gas grill, or move the meat over indirect heat on a charcoal grill. Close the lid and cook for approximately 14 more minutes for medium-rare.

To make the oil, heat a small saucepan over high heat and add the olive oil. When the oil is hot, add the garlic and cook until browned, stirring to keep the slices from sticking together. When the garlic is golden brown, add the rosemary leaves. Remove the pan from the heat and stir the oil with a small spoon.

Cook the steak as you would above and, when ready, remove from the grill. Using a clean cutting board, cut the bone away from the steak and continue to slice the steak into 6 large slices. Arrange the slices on a platter, reheat the oil, and spoon the oil over the steak. Garnish with the rosemary and serve immediately.

Barbecue-Braised Beef Short Ribs

SERVES 4

¼ cup corn oil or other neutral oil such as grapeseed or canola

4 pounds beef short ribs, cut into individual ribs about 4 inches long

Kosher salt

Freshly ground black pepper

½ cup finely diced white onions

¼ cup thinly sliced garlic (from about 12 cloves)

1 cup red wine vinegar

1 tablespoon finely chopped canned chipotle in adobo

2 cups strong decaf coffee

2½ cups canned crushed tomatoes

¼ cup packed light brown sugar

1 cup orange juice

¼ cup finely chopped fresh cilantro leaves

walzog on short ribs

When you're shopping for short ribs, you want them to be as plump as possible and you want some fat on them. Don't ask the butcher to trim them or he may cut away too much fat. You can trim most of it off, but leave a little on the ribs so they stay juicy.

Preheat the oven to 375°F. Heat 2 tablespoons of the oil in a sauté pan. Season the ribs with 2 tablespoons salt and 2 teaspoons pepper. Add the ribs to the pan and brown them for about 10 minutes, until all of the ribs are very brown and well seared. Heat the remaining 2 tablespoons oil in a heavy-bottomed pot over high heat. Sauté the onions and garlic until lightly browned, 4 to 5 minutes. Add the vinegar, chipotle, and coffee. Cook over medium-high heat until reduced by one-third, 10 to 12 minutes. Add the tomatoes, sugar, orange juice, and cilantro and cook for 20 minutes. Add the ribs. Put the pot in the oven, uncovered, and braise the short ribs for 2 hours or until fork tender.

Remove the pot from the oven. Preheat the broiler. Pull the short rib meat from the bones and discard the bones. Put the meat in an ovenproof casserole. Degrease the sauce and smother the ribs with the sauce, using it all. Broil until the sauce thickens and begins to cling to the ribs, 8 to 10 minutes. To serve, divide the ribs among individual plates or serve family style from a platter.

Chopped Vegetable Salad with Smoked Bacon and Red Wine Vinaigrette

My father used to make a super-tangy vinaigrette that we ate so much when I was a kid that I feel like it's become part of my DNA. I've borrowed it to dress this crisp and crunchy salad of haricots verts, cucumber, tomatoes, and onions. This is the only dressing that I shake in the bottle, just like Dad used to do. This salad uses a lot of dressing. To keep everything crisp, don't dress it until the last second. If you have any vegetarians at the table, serve the smoked bacon on the side in a small bowl.

SERVES 6 TO 8

Kosher salt

1½ cups haricots verts cut into ¾-inch pieces (from about 6 ounces beans)

 1 pound double-smoked slab bacon, skinned and cut crosswise into ¼- to ½-inch pieces

 3 cups finely chopped mixed baby greens

 6 cups finely chopped hearts of romaine lettuce (from about 2 heads lettuce)

1½ cups peeled, diced cucumber

 2 cups cored, diced beefsteak tomatoes (from about 3 medium tomatoes)

1½ cups diced red onions

Red Wine Vinaigrette (recipe follows)

Bring a pot of lightly salted water to a boil. Fill a large bowl halfway with ice water. Add the beans to the boiling water and blanch them for 5 to 6 minutes. Use a slotted spoon to transfer them to the ice water to cool them and stop the cooking. Drain and set aside. Put the bacon in a pot with 2 cups water. Bring to a boil over medium heat and let boil until the water evaporates, approximately 15 minutes. Let the bacon fry in the fat that remains in the pot until crisp, approximately 8 more minutes, stirring to keep it from scorching. Use tongs or a slotted spoon to transfer the bacon to a paper-towel-lined plate to drain. To serve, put the bacon, haricots verts, greens, lettuce, cucumber, tomatoes, and onions in a bowl. Drizzle with the vinaigrette, toss well, divide among 6 to 8 plates, and serve at once.

The New American
Steakhouse
Cookbook

DAVID WALZOG AND
ANDREW FRIEDMAN

BONUS POINT

You can substitute other vegetables, such as asparagus, summer squash, and sweet peppers, for the ones in this salad. Trim and/or seed them, cut into ¾-inch pieces, and blanch each separately following the technique for blanching the haricots verts.

Red Wine Vinaigrette

MAKES 1¾ CUPS

1¼ cups extra virgin olive oil

½ cup red wine vinegar

1 tablespoon kosher salt

1 tablespoon garlic powder

½ teaspoon freshly ground black pepper

Put all of the ingredients in a jar or bottle. Close tightly and shake well. Serve at room temperature.

walzog on the best bacon

Use a highly smoked slab bacon for this recipe. I love the bacon from North Country Smoke House in Claremont, New Hampshire (ncsmokehouse.com).

Steamed Littleneck Clams, Roasted Tomato Broth, and Grilled Sourdough Bread

I've always believed that one of the best parts of eating clams is dunking hunks of bread into the broth. So I created a powerfully flavored broth for that very purpose. Of course, it also makes the clams delicious, but dipping that bread into the bowl is still one of my favorite indulgences.

SERVES 4

- 12 plum tomatoes, cored and split lengthwise
- ¾ cup plus 2 tablespoons extra virgin olive oil, plus more for drizzling bread
- 5 fresh thyme sprigs plus 2 teaspoons chopped fresh thyme leaves
- ¼ cup thinly sliced garlic (from 5 or 6 large cloves)

Kosher salt

Freshly ground black pepper

- ½ cup dry white wine
- 2½ pounds littleneck clams (about 24 clams), cleaned and rinsed
- 2 teaspoons grated lemon zest
- 1 loaf sourdough bread, cut into 1-inch-thick slices
- 1 tablespoon cold unsalted butter

Preheat the oven to 325°F.

Lay the tomato halves on a baking sheet, cut side up. Drizzle with ¼ cup of the olive oil and scatter the thyme sprigs, 2 tablespoons of the sliced garlic, 1½ teaspoons salt, and 1 teaspoon pepper over the tomatoes. Drizzle ¼ cup water onto the baking sheet around the tomatoes, which will help keep them moist while roasting. Roast the tomatoes until slightly browned and dry, 25 to 30 minutes. Remove the sheet from the oven and transfer everything to a bowl. Add 1 cup water and ½ cup extra virgin olive oil. Cover and let steep for 30 minutes. Strain through a fine-mesh strainer set over a bowl, pressing down on the solids to extract as much flavorful liquid as possible. You should have about 1¾ cups tomato broth. Discard the solids and reserve the broth.

editor's note

Turn this into a hearty main course by adding mussels and chunks of firm-fleshed white fish such as snapper, cod or halibut.

BREAK POINT

The broth can be covered and refrigerated for up to 72 hours.

Preheat the broiler.

Heat a large sauté pan over medium-high heat on the stove. Add the remaining 2 tablespoons oil and, when hot, sauté the remaining 2 tablespoons garlic until browned, 1 to 2 minutes. Remove from the heat and add the white wine. Place the pan back on the stovetop and add the clams, lemon zest, thyme leaves, tomato broth, 2 teaspoons salt, and 1 teaspoon pepper. Cover and steam over high heat until the clams open, 5 to 6 minutes.

Meanwhile, arrange the bread on a baking sheet in a single layer. Drizzle with extra virgin olive oil and place under the broiler until just beginning to turn golden and crisp, 1 to 2 minutes per side. Remove from the oven and set aside.

Remove the cover from the sauté pan and discard any clams that have not opened. Gently stir in the butter.

To serve, divide the clams and broth among 4 wide, deep bowls and serve the bread alongside. Make sure to have an empty bowl or two handy for empty shells.

BONUS POINT

For a more communal experience, serve the clams and broth from a giant bowl and let everyone serve themselves.

The New American Steakhouse Cookbook

DAVID WALZOG AND
ANDREW FRIEDMAN

BEST OF THE BEST EXCLUSIVE

Crab and Avocado Salad with Creamy Herb Dressing

4 SERVINGS

½ cup crème fraîche

1½ tablespoons fresh lemon juice

2 teaspoons finely grated lemon zest

2 anchovy fillets, drained

1½ tablespoons capers, drained

½ teaspoon kosher salt

Pinch of cayenne pepper

2 tablespoons finely chopped chervil

2 tablespoons finely chopped flat-leaf parsley

1 tablespoon finely chopped dill

1 tablespoon finely chopped tarragon

1 pound jumbo lump crabmeat, picked over

1 head of frisée (½ pound), torn into bite-size pieces (6 cups)

1 ripe Hass avocado—peeled, pitted and cut into ⅓-inch dice

1. In a blender, puree the crème fraîche, lemon juice, lemon zest, anchovies, capers, salt and cayenne until smooth. Transfer to a small bowl and stir in the chervil, parsley, dill and tarragon. Cover and refrigerate the dressing for at least 2 hours or overnight.

2. In a medium bowl, toss the crab with ½ cup of the dressing. In a large bowl, toss the frisée with the remaining dressing. Transfer the frisée to plates, top with the crab salad and diced avocado and serve.

Autumn Squash Soup with Country
Ham and Garlic Croutes, p. 258

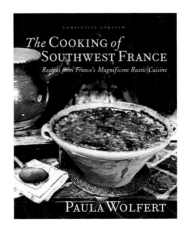

The Cooking of Southwest France

by Paula Wolfert

When Paula Wolfert debuted *The Cooking of Southwest France* in 1983, she introduced America to all kinds of new flavors—like duck fat, gizzards and cèpes. "I went to torturous extremes to make the recipes taste just as they did in France," says Wolfert. "I wanted them to taste like the truth." Luckily, authentic French ingredients are now much easier to find, inspiring Wolfert to spend a year retesting her classic recipes and adding 30 new ones. The result is an updated edition thick with terrific, rustic, sometimes extremely elaborate, dishes that still taste like the truth.

Published by John Wiley & Sons, 480 pages, $37.50.

BEST RECIPES

Autumn Squash Soup with Country Ham and Garlic Croutes
258

Ragout of Duck Legs with White Onions and Prunes
261

Fillet of Beef with Roquefort Sauce and Mixed Nuts
265

Find more recipes by Paula Wolfert at
foodandwine.com/wolfert

Autumn Squash Soup with Country Ham and Garlic Croutes

Crème de Potiron

This fall soup is served with hot crisp rounds of French baguette topped with a good rubbing of garlic. To enhance the flavor of the squash, I roast it in the oven to preserve its natural sweetness. This soup reheats well, retaining its velvety texture and great savor.

SERVES 6

- 1½ to 2 pounds butternut, kabocha, or buttercup squash
- 2 tablespoons extra virgin olive oil
- 2 tablespoons rendered duck fat or butter
- ½ cup chopped onion
- ½ pound Yukon gold potatoes, peeled and cubed
- 3 garlic cloves, peeled and halved
- 4 cups unsalted chicken stock (store-bought or homemade—recipe follows)

Salt and freshly ground pepper

Freshly grated nutmeg

- 1 cup heavy cream

Pinch of *piment d'Espelette* or any moderately hot red pepper

2½ ounces jambon de Bayonne, Serrano ham, or prosciutto, trimmed of fat and cut into thin ribbons

- 6 thin slices of stale baguette
- 2 tablespoons minced fresh chives

1. Preheat the oven to 400°F. Wash the squash, halve lengthwise, and lay cut side down on a foil-lined baking sheet. Bake about 30 minutes, until soft. Turn the squash over, turn off the heat, and let the squash finish cooking and browning in the hot, turned-off oven for 10 minutes longer. Remove the squash and let stand until cool enough to handle. Scoop out the seeds and cut away the skin; discard.

2. Meanwhile, heat the oil and half the duck fat in a heavy 4-quart pot over moderately low heat. Add the onion, potatoes, and 1 of the garlic cloves and slowly cook the vegetables until soft and pale golden, 10 to 15 minutes. Add the chicken broth and simmer for 30 minutes.

3. Scrape the roasted squash into a food processor or blender. Add a few tablespoons of the hot soup broth and puree until velvet-smooth. Working in batches, puree the contents of the pot. Or if you have an immersion blender, puree the soup directly in the pot. Season with salt, pepper, and nutmeg to taste. Add the cream and bring to a boil. Reduce the heat and simmer for 5 minutes to blend the flavors.

4. In a medium skillet, heat the remaining duck fat with a pinch each of black pepper and piment d'Espelette. Add the ribbons of ham and the rounds of bread and sauté over moderately high heat until slightly crisp, about 2 minutes. Generously rub the bread with the remaining garlic. Serve the soup garnished with the ham, toasted bread, and chives.

Chicken Stock
Fond de Volaille
Use this rich stock for soups, pot-au-feu, and some stews. It can be stored in the refrigerator for up to 3 days or frozen in covered containers for up to 3 months.

MAKES 2 QUARTS

 5 pounds chicken necks, backs, and wings, plus leftover roasted carcasses, if available

2 or 3 chicken gizzards

 1 veal shank or a few marrowbones (optional)

 2 onions, halved

Green tops from 2 or 3 leeks

 2 small celery ribs, halved

 1 carrot, halved

Peel and seeds from 2 tomatoes or 1 plum tomato, quartered (see Note that follows)

 2 garlic cloves

 2 whole cloves

1. Place the chicken parts, gizzards, and veal shank or marrowbones (if you have them) in a large stockpot. Cover with warm water and quickly bring to a boil over high heat. Boil vigorously for 3 minutes. Drain; rinse the bones and return them to the pot.

2. Cover with 6 quarts cold water; slowly bring to a boil. Skim off any scum that surfaces until only a small amount of foam rises to the top. Add the onions, leek greens, celery, carrot, tomato or tomatoes, garlic, and cloves. Return to a boil. Reduce the heat to low, partially cover the pot, and simmer slowly, without disturbing, for 4 to 5 hours.

3. Ladle the stock through a colander into a deep bowl. Then ladle it again through a strainer lined with several thicknesses of damp cheesecloth. Skim the fat off the top. If you have time, chill the stock, then scrape off all the congealed fat.

4. Put the degreased stock in a large, heavy saucepan and bring to a boil. Slide the pan half off the heat and cook at a slow boil, skimming, for 25 to 30 minutes, or until the stock is reduced to 2 quarts.

NOTE Peel and seeds from fresh tomatoes will flavor the stock as well as attract scum. Use the best part of the tomato for some other purpose.

Ragout of Duck Legs with White Onions and Prunes

Ragoût de Cuisses de Caneton aux Petits Oignons et aux Pruneaux

Duck breasts have become so popular that people often wonder what to do with the legs. One solution is to use them in this excellent dish, which relies on a good hearty wine for background richness. The slow simmering and the degreasing make this version of the dish much lighter than others. The duck can be cooked in advance, then gently reheated. The addition of bread fried in olive oil actually rounds out the flavor of the dish; don't leave it out. This is one of my favorite duck recipes. Inspired by a recipe from Lucien Vanel.

SERVES 4

- 12 extra large pitted prunes
- 2 cups hot tea, preferably linden or orange pekoe
- 4 Pekin duck legs, drumsticks and thighs separated
- 5 ounces thickly sliced ventrèche or pancetta, cut into 2-by-⅛-inch strips (lardons) and blanched
- 3 garlic cloves, peeled
- ½ teaspoon salt
- ¼ teaspoon freshly ground pepper
- Pinch of dried thyme leaves, crumbled
- 1 large red onion, thinly sliced
- 1 tablespoon red wine vinegar
- 1 tablespoon Dijon mustard
- 2¼ cups full-bodied red wine, such as California Petite Sirah or a French Côtes-du-Rhône
- 1½ cups unsalted chicken stock (store-bought or homemade—page 259)
- 3 medium carrots, peeled, halved crosswise, then lengthwise
- 18 small white onions (about 1 inch in diameter)
- 2 tablespoons unsalted butter
- 1½ teaspoons sugar
- 8 thin baguette slices, toasted
- Chopped fresh flat-leaf parsley

wolfert on flavoring prunes

I like to soak the prunes in tea rather than just water because it adds flavor. There's something in tea, maybe the tannins, that brings out the flavor in the prunes. Maybe it's an old wives' tale. Maybe some scientist will prove it is bunk, but that's how I like to do it.

Ragout of Duck Legs with
White Onions and Prunes

1. Soak the prunes in the hot tea for 2 hours. Drain, reserving the prunes and discarding the liquid.

2. Trim off the loose fat from the duck legs and render it with 2 tablespoons water. Strain, reserving 2 tablespoons for this dish. Keep the remainder for some other purpose. Score the skin of the duck with the point of a small knife. Wipe off excess moisture.

3. Heat the duck fat in a heavy nonreactive skillet over moderate heat. Add the blanched lardons and fry, turning occasionally, until light brown, about 4 minutes. Remove with a slotted spoon and drain on paper towels. Reserve the drippings in the skillet. Transfer the lardons to a 4-quart flameproof casserole.

4. Add the duck pieces to the reserved drippings in the skillet and cook over moderately high heat, turning occasionally, until well browned, about 10 minutes. Briefly drain the duck on paper towels and add to the lardons in the casserole. Add 2 of the garlic cloves, the salt, pepper, and thyme and toss to mix.

5. Pour off all but 2 tablespoons fat from the skillet. Add the red onion to the skillet and sauté over moderate heat, stirring frequently, until lightly browned, about 5 minutes. Remove the onion with a slotted spoon, drain thoroughly on paper towels, and add to the casserole.

6. Pour off all the fat from the skillet; whisk in the vinegar, mustard, and ⅓ cup of the wine. Bring to a boil, scraping up any brown bits clinging to the pan. Reduce to a glaze. Add another ⅓ cup wine and reduce again to develop a stronger, deeper color in the sauce.

7. Pour the deglazing liquid from the skillet, the remaining wine, and the stock into the casserole; heat to boiling. Reduce the heat and simmer, uncovered, for 5 minutes, skimming. Add the carrots. Cover the casserole and simmer over low heat until the duck is tender, about 1½ hours; or cook in a preheated 300°F oven. (This recipe can be prepared up to this step. Cool, cover, and refrigerate.)

8. Cut an X in root end of each small onion. Blanch for 2 minutes. Drain and rinse under cold water until cool enough to handle. Peel the onions, leaving on enough root and stem end so the onion won't fall apart.

9. Combine the onions, butter, sugar, and ½ cup water in a medium skillet. Bring to a simmer over moderate heat and cook, stirring occasionally, until the water has evaporated, about 6 minutes. Reduce the heat to low and continue to cook, shaking the pan occasionally, until the onions are tender and nicely browned, about 8 minutes.

10. About 20 minutes before serving, add the prunes to the ragout and gently reheat. Transfer the duck pieces to a warm platter; surround with the prunes, carrots, and onions. Sprinkle the lardons over the duck; tent loosely with foil. Strain the sauce from the casserole through a fine-mesh sieve into a small saucepan, pressing on the solids with the back of a spoon to extract as much liquid as possible. Skim off any fat from the sauce. Bring to a boil and set the saucepan half on and half off the heat. Cook at a slow boil, skimming, for 10 minutes, or until the liquid is reduced enough to coat a spoon lightly. Spoon the sauce over the duck and vegetables, garnish with parsley and serve at once with the toasted baguette slices.

NOTES

To save time, defrosted frozen baby onions can be substituted for fresh here. Skip Step 8 and glaze as directed in Step 9.

If substituting Muscovy or Moulard duck legs, please note they need to cook longer, as much as 1 hour.

Fillet of Beef with Roquefort Sauce and Mixed Nuts

Filet de Boeuf au Roquefort

This combination is a specialty of the town of St.-Juéry in the Tarn. The brilliant sauce is the creation of Gascon chef André Daguin. The method of cooking and racking the fillet is my way of handling roasts and thick steaks.

SERVES 4 TO 5

- 1 center-cut beef tenderloin (2 pounds; trimmed weight 1¾ pounds)

Salt and freshly ground pepper

Grapeseed or peanut oil

- 1 teaspoon rendered duck or goose fat or clarified butter
- 1 tablespoon minced shallots
- 3 tablespoons dry Madeira or imported ruby port
- ½ cup demi-glace, store-bought or homemade (recipe follows) or 1½ cups unsalted meat stock reduced to ½ cup
- 1½ ounces creamy Roquefort cheese
- 3 tablespoons unsalted butter, plus more if necessary
- 2 tablespoons crème fraîche or whipped heavy cream
- 2 tablespoons lightly toasted pine nuts
- 2 tablespoons lightly toasted walnut pieces
- 2 tablespoons lightly toasted sliced blanched almonds
- 1 tablespoon chopped fresh flat-leaf parsley

1. Lightly sprinkle meat with salt and pepper. Rub a little oil over the beef. Loosely cover with plastic wrap and refrigerate until 1 hour before cooking. Pat the roast dry with paper towels.

2. In a large heavy skillet, preferably enameled cast-iron, heat 2 teaspoons oil and the fat until very hot. Sear the meat over high heat, turning, until browned all over, about 4 minutes total. Transfer the roast to a wire rack; let rest for a minimum of 20 minutes.

3. Throw out the cooking fat. Add the chopped shallots and Madeira or port to the skillet; boil until reduced to a glaze. Add the demi-glace or reduced stock and bring to a boil. Reduce to a syrupy consistency. Set aside.

4. Crush the Roquefort and the butter to a smooth, creamy paste. Taste the mixture; if it's too salty, add another ½ to 1 tablespoon butter. Cover and refrigerate.

5. About 30 minutes before serving, preheat the oven to 450°F. Roast the beef fillets to 120°F or for 17 minutes for "blue" (very rare); to 125°F or for 18 minutes for rare; or to 135°F or for 19 minutes for medium-rare.

6. Meanwhile, gently reheat the syrupy sauce in the skillet. Divide the Roquefort butter into 4 or 5 chunks and swirl into the sauce, one by one. Remove from the heat and fold the crème fraîche or whipped cream into the sauce.

7. Spoon the sauce onto a heated serving platter. Slice meat and arrange, overlapping, on the platter. Surround with the toasted nuts mixed with the parsley. Serve at once.

Demi-Glace
Demi-Glace

MAKES 2½ CUPS

  8 to 10 pounds veal bones
  2 to 3 pounds chicken carcasses, plus 1 heart and 1 gizzard
Several chunks of fatty veal (optional)
  3 tablespoons rendered duck or goose fat or butter
  2 ounces fatty cured ham, chopped (optional)
  2 medium carrots, chopped
  2 medium onions, chopped, plus 1 onion, halved
  1 leek, split and sliced (white and green parts separated)
  1 small celery rib, sliced
  6 sprigs of parsley
  1 head of garlic, halved horizontally
  1 large tomato, halved, with skin and seeds
  1 imported bay leaf
  ¼ teaspoon freshly grated nutmeg

1. Crack the veal bones and chicken carcasses with a cleaver into very small pieces or have the butcher do this for you. Place them in a deep stockpot, cover with warm water, and quickly bring to a boil. Boil hard for 3 minutes. Drain, rinse, and return to the pot.

2. Cover the bones with 6 quarts cold water. Add the fatty pieces of veal if you have them. Slowly bring to a boil over moderate heat, skimming off the scum as it rises to the top. Simmer, skimming, for 1 hour.

3. Meanwhile, in a large skillet, heat the fat. Add the ham, carrots, and chopped onions. Cover and cook over low heat for 10 minutes to sweat the vegetables.

4. Add the white parts of the leek and the celery. Raise the heat to moderate and cook the vegetables, stirring occasionally, until lightly browned, about 15 minutes. Caramelize the cut sides of the halved onion by placing them close to burner flames or under a hot broiler until blackened.

5. When bones have simmered for 1 hour and the liquid is clear, add the browned vegetables, caramelized onion, leek greens, parsley, garlic, tomato, bay leaf, and nutmeg. Return to a boil, reduce the heat to low, and simmer, uncovered, skimming from time to time without stirring, for at least 4 hours.

6. Strain the stock through a colander into a deep bowl, discarding the solids. Then ladle the stock through a sieve lined with several thicknesses of damp cheesecloth. Chill uncovered until the fat congeals, then scrape it all off.

7. Return the degreased stock to a clean heavy saucepan. Bring to a boil. Slide the pan half off the heat and cook at a slow boil, skimming, until reduced to 2½ cups, about 1 hour. The demi-glace should just lightly coat a spoon.

editor's note

Wolfert adds 2 tablespoons crème fraîche or whipped cream to the sauce here to thicken it. She argues that this isn't as decadent as it sounds since crème fraîche and whipped cream have about half the fat of butter.

Buttery and Soft Chocolate
Cake for a Crowd, p. 270

Chocolate Chocolate

by Lisa Yockelson

"I started keeping a recipe file when I was seven," says journalist and cookbook author Lisa Yockelson. That file has grown into 13 books, including *Chocolate Chocolate,* a 500-page tome over six years in the making. With more than 200 recipes for cakes, cookies, bars, waffles and pancakes, Yockelson celebrates chocolate in all its varieties—white, milk, semisweet, dark and bitter. She's inventive, too—she even adds store-bought candy to some of her recipes, like Heath and Butterfinger bars.

Published by John Wiley & Sons, 512 pages, $45.

BEST RECIPES

Buttery and Soft
Chocolate Cake for
a Crowd
270

Layered Blondie Squares
273

Giant Chocolate Chip
Coffee Cake Muffins
275

**BEST OF THE BEST
EXCLUSIVE**

Large and Luscious
Two-Chip
Oatmeal Cookies
277

Buttery and Soft Chocolate Cake for a Crowd

yockelson on the best brown sugar

I like the depth of flavor that light brown sugar brings to this batter, plus it makes the cake nice and moist. Don't be tempted to use dark brown sugar, however; the flavor is too prominent.

Butter and sour cream combine to develop a lush framework for a batter that bakes into an exceedingly tender, feathery, yet moist chocolate cake. Its composition is downy rather than compact and, as chocolate desserts go, texturally lighter than any of the flourless chocolate cakes in this book, but no less rich. This cake calls out for an abundant stretch of frosting, and when nothing less than that will do, the Soft and Luxurious Chocolate Frosting that follows is simply ideal.

ONE 13-BY-9-INCH CAKE, CREATING 20 SQUARES

BUTTER AND SOUR CREAM CHOCOLATE BATTER

- 4 ounces unsweetened chocolate, chopped
- ½ cup plus 2 tablespoons and 1½ teaspoons water
- 2 cups bleached cake flour
- 1 teaspoon baking powder
- 1 teaspoon baking soda
- ½ teaspoon salt
- ½ pound (16 tablespoons or 2 sticks) unsalted butter, softened
- 1¼ cups firmly packed light brown sugar
- ¼ cup plus 2 tablespoons granulated sugar
- 3 large eggs
- 1 large egg yolk
- 2 teaspoons vanilla extract
- 1 cup sour cream

FROSTING

Soft and Luxurious Chocolate Frosting (recipe follows)

PREHEAT THE OVEN TO 350°F. Lightly grease the inside of a 13-by-9-by-2-inch baking pan with shortening and dust with flour.

MIX THE BATTER Place the chocolate and water in a small, heavy saucepan (preferably enameled cast iron) and set over low heat. As the chocolate begins to melt, stir it from time to time with a wooden spoon or flat paddle.

When the chocolate has melted, stir slowly to blend until smooth. By the time you need to use it, it should be slightly warm and the texture of thick pudding.

Sift the flour, baking powder, baking soda, and salt onto a sheet of waxed paper.

Cream the butter in the large bowl of a freestanding electric mixer on moderate speed for 2 to 3 minutes. Add the light brown sugar in 2 additions, beating for 1 minute after each portion is added. Add the granulated sugar and beat for 1 minute longer. Add the eggs, one at a time, beating for 45 seconds after each addition. Beat in the egg yolk. Blend in the chocolate mixture and vanilla extract. The mixture may look slightly curdled at this point—OK—but will be restored once the sifted mixture and sour cream are added to complete the batter. On low speed, alternately add the sifted mixture in 3 additions with the sour cream in 2 additions, beginning and ending with the sifted mixture. Scrape down the sides of the mixing bowl frequently to keep the batter even-textured. The batter will be soft, light, and very creamy.

Spoon the batter into the prepared pan and spread evenly. Smooth the top with a rubber spatula.

BAKE, COOL, AND FROST THE CAKE Bake the cake in the preheated oven for 35 to 40 minutes, or until risen, set, and toothpick inserted in the center withdraws clean. The baked cake will pull away slightly from the sides of the pan. Cool the cake in the pan on a rack. Spread the frosting over the cake. Let the cake stand for 1 hour before cutting into squares for serving.

Bake and serve within 1 day.

Soft and Luxurious Chocolate Frosting

Indulgent in all the best ways—buttery, chocolate-endowed, creamy.

ABOUT 4 CUPS FROSTING

6 tablespoons (¾ stick) unsalted butter, softened
4 ounces unsweetened chocolate, melted and cooled to tepid
Large pinch of salt
2½ teaspoons vanilla extract
⅔ cup milk, heated to tepid
5½ cups confectioners' sugar, sifted

Place the butter in the bowl of a heavy-duty freestanding electric mixer fitted with the flat paddle attachment. Beat on moderate speed for 1 minute. Blend in the melted chocolate, the salt, the vanilla extract, half of the milk, and 1½ cups of the confectioners' sugar. Add the balance of the milk and beat for 1 minute. Add half of the remaining confectioners' sugar and beat for 1 minute, or until smooth. Add the balance of the confectioners' sugar, beat on low speed to blend, then beat on moderately high speed until very creamy and somewhat lightened in texture, about 3 minutes. Scrape down the sides of the mixing bowl frequently to keep the frosting even-textured.

Adjust the texture of the frosting to soft spreading consistency, as needed, by adding additional teaspoons of milk or tablespoons of confectioners' sugar.

STUDY This frosting is especially suited for spreading on the top of a sheet cake because it is so soft and creamy. The qualities that make it so enticing for spreading over a single layer preclude it from being used for piping, when a stiffer consistency is desired.

Layered Blondie Squares

16 SQUARES

CHOCOLATE COOKIE LAYER

8 tablespoons (1 stick) unsalted butter, melted and cooled to tepid

1½ cups plus 2 tablespoons chocolate cookie crumbs (such as crumbs made from Nabisco Famous Chocolate Wafers)

CHOCOLATE CHIP BATTER

¾ cup plus 2 tablespoons bleached all-purpose flour

¼ cup bleached cake flour

¼ teaspoon baking powder

⅛ teaspoon salt

8 tablespoons (1 stick) unsalted butter, softened

½ cup firmly packed dark brown sugar

3 tablespoons granulated sugar

1 large egg

1 large egg yolk

1½ teaspoons vanilla extract

1 cup plus 2 tablespoons semisweet chocolate chips

¾ cup sweetened flaked coconut

PREHEAT THE OVEN AND PREPARE THE BAKING PAN Preheat the oven to 350°F. Film the inside of an 8-by-8-by-2-inch baking pan with nonstick cooking spray.

MIX, BAKE, AND COOL THE COOKIE LAYER Pour the melted butter into the prepared pan. Spoon the cookie crumbs evenly over the bottom of the pan and press down lightly with the underside of a small offset metal spatula so that the crumbs absorb the butter. Bake the cookie layer in the preheated oven for 4 minutes. Place the baking pan on a rack. Cool for 10 minutes.

MIX THE BATTER Sift the all-purpose flour, cake flour, baking powder, and salt onto a sheet of waxed paper.

Cream the butter in the large bowl of a freestanding electric mixer on moderately low speed for 2 minutes. Add the dark brown sugar and beat for 2 minutes. Add the granulated sugar and beat for 1 minute longer. Blend in the egg, egg yolk,

yockelson on the right flour

It's a good idea to track down cake flour for this recipe. I like it because it softens the crumb of the batter and that means the squares stay moister longer.

and vanilla extract. On low speed, add the sifted mixture in 2 additions, beating until the particles of flour are absorbed. Stir in the chocolate chips and coconut.

Spoon the batter in large dollops on the cookie crumb layer. Carefully spread the batter over the cookie layer, using a flexible palette knife or spatula and gentle, short strokes.

BAKE, COOL, AND CUT THE SWEET Bake the sweet for 25 minutes, or until the blondie topping is set (the center should be stable, not wobbly) and light golden on top. Cool the sweet in the pan on a rack. With a small sharp knife, cut the sweet into quarters, then cut each quarter into 4 squares. Remove the squares from the baking pan, using a small offset metal spatula. Store in an airtight tin.

Bake and serve within 2 days.

Layered Blondie
Squares

Giant Chocolate Chip Coffee Cake Muffins

10 MUFFINS

CHOCOLATE CHIP AND WALNUT TOPPING

¾ cup semisweet chocolate chips

⅔ cup chopped walnuts

3 tablespoons firmly packed light brown sugar

3 tablespoons unsalted butter, melted and cooled

CHOCOLATE CHIP BATTER

3 cups bleached all-purpose flour

2¼ teaspoons baking powder

¼ teaspoon baking soda

¾ teaspoon salt

1⅓ cups semisweet chocolate chips

12 tablespoons (1½ sticks) unsalted butter, softened

⅔ cup plus 1 tablespoon firmly packed light brown sugar

⅓ cup granulated sugar

3 large eggs

2½ teaspoons vanilla extract

1 ounce unsweetened chocolate, melted and cooled

¾ cup milk combined with ¼ cup light (table) cream

Confectioners' sugar, for sifting on top of the baked muffins (optional)

PREHEAT THE OVEN TO 375°F. Line the inside of 10 jumbo muffin/cupcake cups (6 cups to a pan, each cup measuring 4 inches in diameter and 1¾ inches deep, with a capacity of 1⅛ cups) with ovenproof baking paper liners. Or film the inside of each cup with nonstick cooking spray.

MIX THE TOPPING Mix the chocolate chips, walnuts, light brown sugar, and melted butter in a small bowl.

MIX THE BATTER Sift the flour, baking powder, baking soda, and salt onto a sheet of waxed paper. In a small bowl, toss the chocolate chips with 2½ teaspoons of the sifted mixture.

yockelson on chocolate chips

It's important to toss the chocolate chips in flour before you incorporate them into the batter because this prevents them from sinking to the bottom of the muffin.

Cream the butter in the large bowl of a freestanding electric mixer on moderately low speed for 3 minutes. Add the light brown sugar and beat for 2 minutes; add the granulated sugar and beat for 2 minutes longer. Beat in the eggs, one at a time, mixing for 30 seconds after each addition. Blend in the vanilla extract and the melted chocolate. On low speed, alternately add the sifted ingredients in 3 additions with the milk-cream mixture in 2 additions, beginning and ending with the sifted mixture. Scrape down the sides of the mixing bowl frequently to keep the batter even-textured. Stir in the chocolate chips.

FILL THE MUFFIN CUPS AND TOP Divide the batter among the prepared cups, mounding it slightly. Sprinkle a little of the topping over each of the muffins.

BAKE AND COOL THE MUFFINS Bake the muffins in the preheated oven for 25 minutes, or until risen, set, and a toothpick inserted into the center of each muffin withdraws clean (if you bump into a milk chocolate chip, it will be stained—OK).

Place the muffin pans on cooling racks and let them stand for 20 minutes. Carefully remove the muffins and place on cooling racks. Dust the tops lightly with confectioners' sugar, if you wish. Cool. Serve the muffins freshly baked.

Bake and serve within 1 day.

STUDY Just 1 ounce of melted unsweetened chocolate tinges the muffin batter enough to bring out the flavor of all those chocolate chips.

Allowing the baked muffins to remain in the pans for 20 minutes before unmolding maintains their shape.

The batter for the muffins can also be baked in jumbo "crown top" muffin cups (6 cups to a pan, each cup measuring 3¼ inches in diameter and 2 inches deep, with a capacity of a scant 1 cup). To prepare the pans, film the inside of each cup with nonstick cooking spray.

BEST OF THE BEST EXCLUSIVE

Large and Luscious Two-Chip Oatmeal Cookies

MAKES 20 FOUR-INCH COOKIES

1	cup plus 2 tablespoons all-purpose flour
½	teaspoon baking soda
⅛	teaspoon baking powder
¼	teaspoon salt
1½	sticks unsalted butter, at room temperature
½	cup plus 2 tablespoons packed light brown sugar
½	cup granulated sugar
1	large egg
1	large egg white
1½	teaspoons pure vanilla extract
1½	cups quick-cooking rolled oats
1	cup semisweet chocolate chips
½	cup white chocolate chips
¾	cup sweetened flaked coconut

editor's note

Yockelson likes this recipe because the cookie dough can be made ahead of time. The dough can be frozen for up to one month or stored in the refrigerator for up to three days.

1. In a medium bowl, whisk the flour with the baking soda, baking powder and salt. In a large bowl, using an electric mixer, beat the butter with the brown sugar at medium speed until blended. Beat in the granulated sugar and beat until light and fluffy, about 2 minutes. Beat in the whole egg, egg white and vanilla. At low speed, beat in the dry ingredients in 2 additions. With a large wooden spoon, mix in the oats, semisweet and white chocolate chips and the coconut. Cover the cookie dough and refrigerate for 1 hour, until chilled.

2. Preheat the oven to 375°. Line 3 large baking sheets with parchment paper. Using a 1½-ounce ice cream scoop or rounded tablespoon, spoon mounds of dough onto the prepared baking sheets, at least 3 inches apart. Bake the cookies for about 14 minutes until golden and just set. Let the cookies cool on the baking sheets for 5 minutes, then transfer them to a rack to cool completely.

MAKE AHEAD The cookies can be stored in an airtight container for up to 3 days.

Credits

Mangoes & Curry Leaves
Culinary Travels Through the Great Subcontinent
Excerpted from *Mangoes & Curry Leaves*.
Copyright © 2005 by Jeffrey Alford and Naomi
Duguid. Photographs copyright © 2005 by
Richard Jung. Used by permission of Artisan,
a division of Workman Publishing Co., Inc.,
New York. All rights reserved.

Molto Italiano
327 Simple Italian Recipes to Cook at Home
From *Molto Italiano* by Mario Batali. Copyright ©
2005 by Mario Batali. Photographs by Beatriz Da
Costa. Reprinted by permission of HarperCollins
Publishers.

Mexican Everyday
From *Mexican Everyday* by Rick Bayless with
Deann Groen Bayless. Copyright © 2005
by Rick Bayless and Deann Groen Bayless.
Photographs copyright © 2005 by Christopher
Hirsheimer. Used by permission of W. W. Norton
& Company, Inc.

La Cocina de Mamá
The Great Home Cooking of Spain
Excerpted from *La Cocina de Mamá*. Copyright
© 2005 by Penelope Casas. Used by permission
of Broadway Books, a division of Random House,
Inc. All rights reserved. Photographs by Shimon
and Tammar.

Chef, Interrupted
**Delicious Chefs' Recipes That You Can
Actually Make at Home**
From *Chef, Interrupted* by Melissa Clark,
copyright © 2005 by Melissa Clark. Photographs
copyright © 2005 by Tina Rupp. Used by permis-
sion of Clarkson Potter/Publishers, a division of
Random House, Inc.

Everyday Italian
125 Simple and Delicious Recipes
From *Everyday Italian: 125 Simple and Delicious
Recipes* by Giada De Laurentiis, copyright ©
2005 by Giada De Laurentiis. Photographs copyright © 2005 by Victoria Pearson. Used by permission of Clarkson Potter/Publishers, a
division of Random House, Inc.

Paula Deen & Friends
Living It Up, Southern Style
Reprinted with the permission of Simon &
Schuster Adult Publishing Group, from *Paula Deen
& Friends: Living It Up, Southern Style* by Paula
Deen. Photographs by Alan Richardson. Copyright
© 2005 by Paula Deen. Photographs copyright ©
2005 by Alan Richardson. All rights reserved.

Grilling for Life
75 Healthier Ideas for Big Flavor from the Fire
Reprinted with the permission of Scribner, an
imprint of Simon & Schuster Adult Publishing
Group, from *Grilling for Life* by Bobby Flay.
Copyright © 2005 by Boy Meets Grill, Inc. Color
food photographs copyright © 2005 by Gentl &
Hyers. Cover photograph © 2005 by John Dolan.

Eat This Book
Cooking with Global Fresh Flavors
From *Eat This Book: Cooking with Global Fresh
Flavors* by Tyler Florence, copyright © 2005 by
Tyler Florence. Photographs copyright © 2005 by
Petrina Tinslay. Used by permission of Clarkson
Potter/Publishers, a division of Random House, Inc.

Sunday Suppers at Lucques
Seasonal Recipes from Market to Table
From *Sunday Suppers at Lucques* by Suzanne
Goin with Teri Gelber, copyright © 2005 by
Suzanne Goin. Used by permission of Alfred
A. Knopf, a division of Random House, Inc.
Photographs by Shimon and Tammar.

Supper at Richard's Place
Recipes from the New Southern Table
From *Supper at Richard's Place* by Richard Jones.
Copyright © 2005 by Richard Jones. Used by
permission of the licenser, Pelican Publishing
Company, Inc.

Small Bites
**Tapas, Sushi, Mezze, Antipasti, and
Other Finger Foods**
Excerpted from *Small Bites* by Jennifer Joyce.
Copyright © 2005 Dorling Kindersley Limited. Text
copyright © 2005 by Jennifer Joyce. Published in
the United States by DK Publishing, Inc. All rights
reserved. Photographs by Sian Irvine.

Eating Korean
From Barbecue to Kimchi, Recipes from My Home
Excerpted from *Eating Korean* by Cecilia Hae-Jin Lee. Copyright © 2005 by Cecilia Hae-Jin Lee. Reprinted by permission of John Wiley & Sons, Inc. All rights reserved.

Brunch
100 Recipes from Five Points Restaurant
Excerpted from *Brunch* by Marc Meyer and Peter Meehan. © 2005 by Marc Meyer and Peter Meehan. Photographs © 2005 by Ben Fink. Reprinted by permission of Universe Publishing, a division of Rizzoli International Publications, Inc. All rights reserved.

Chocolate Obsession
Confections and Treats to Create and Savor
Excerpted from *Chocolate Obsession* by Michael Recchiuti and Fran Gage. Text copyright © 2005 Michael Recchiuti and Fran Gage. Photographs copyright © 2005 by Maren Caruso. Printed by permission of Stewart, Tabori & Chang. All rights reserved.

Galatoire's Cookbook
Recipes and Family History from the Time-Honored New Orleans Restaurant
From *Galatoire's Cookbook* by Melvin Rodrigue with Jyl Benson, copyright © 2005 by Galatoire's Restaurant. Used by permission of Clarkson Potter/Publishers, a division of Random House, Inc. Photographs by Eugenia Uhl and Louis Sahuc.

Seasoned in the South
Recipes from Crook's Corner and from Home
From *Seasoned in the South: Recipes from Crook's Corner and from Home* by Bill Smith. © 2005 by Bill Smith. Reprinted by permission of Algonquin Books of Chapel Hill.

The Rustic Table
Simple Fare from the World's Kitchens
From *The Rustic Table* by Constance Snow. Copyright © 2005 by Constance Snow. Reprinted by permission of HarperCollins Publishers.

Recipes
A Collection for the Modern Cook
From *Recipes: A Collection for the Modern Cook* by Susan Spungen. Copyright © 2005 by Susan Spungen. Photographs copyright © by Maria Robledo. Foreword copyright © 2005 by Martha Stewart. Reprinted by permission of HarperCollins Publishers. Photographs by Maria Robledo.

Sweet Gratitude
Bake a Thank-You for the Really Important People in Your Life
Excerpted from *Sweet Gratitude*. Copyright © 2005 by Judith Sutton. Watercolor illustrations copyright © 2005 by Mariko Jesse. Used by permission of Artisan, a division of Workman Publishing Co., Inc., New York. All rights reserved.

The Herbal Kitchen
Cooking with Fragrance and Flavor
From *The Herbal Kitchen* by Jerry Traunfeld. Copyright © 2005 by Jerry Traunfeld. Photographs copyright © 2005 by John Granen. Reprinted by permission of HarperCollins Publishers.

The New Spanish Table
300 Recipes of Spain in All Its Glory
Excerpted from *The New Spanish Table*. Copyright © 2005 by Anya von Bremzen. Photographs copyright © 2005 by Susan Goldman. Used by permission of Workman Publishing Co., Inc., New York. All rights reserved.

The New American Steakhouse Cookbook
It's Not Just Meat and Potatoes Anymore
The New American Steakhouse Cookbook by David Walzog and Andrew Friedman. Copyright © 2005 by David Walzog. Printed by permission of Broadway Books, a division of Random House, Inc. All rights reserved. Photographs by Shimon and Tammar Rothstein.

The Cooking of Southwest France
Recipes from France's Magnificent Rustic Cuisine
Reprinted by permission from *The Cooking of Southwest France: Recipes from France's Magnificent Rustic Cuisine* by Paula Wolfert. Published by John Wiley & Sons, Inc. Copyright © 2005 by Paula Wolfert. All rights reserved. Photographs by Christopher Hirsheimer.

Chocolate Chocolate
Reprinted by permission from *Chocolate Chocolate* by Lisa Yockelson. Published by John Wiley & Sons, Inc. Copyright © 2005 by Lisa Yockelson. All rights reserved. Photographs by Ben Fink.

Index

Page numbers in **bold** indicate photographs.

Page numbers in **bold** indicate photographs.